1-to-1 at Home
A Parent's Guide to School-Issued Laptops and Tablets

Jason Brand

HomePage Books is an imprint of the
International Society for Technology in Education

EUGENE, OREGON • WASHINGTON, DC

1-to-1 at Home
A Parent's Guide to School-Issued Laptops and Tablets
Jason Brand

Content © Jason Brand

Paperback edition © 2013 International Society for Technology in Education
World rights reserved. No part of this book may be reproduced or transmitted in any form or by any means—electronic, mechanical, photocopying, recording, or by any information storage or retrieval system—without prior written permission from the publisher. Contact Permissions Editor: www.iste.org/learn/publications/permissions-and-reprints.aspx; permissions@iste.org; fax: 1.541.302.3780.

Director of Book Publishing: *Courtney Burkholder*
Acquisitions Editor: *Jeff V. Bolkan*
Production Editors: *Tina Wells, Lynda Gansel*
Production Coordinator: *Emily Reed*
Graphic Designer: *Signe Landin*
Copy Editor: *Kathy Hamman*
Cover Design: *Signe Landin*
Book Design and Production: *Kerry Lutz*

Library of Congress Cataloging-in-Publication Data

Brand, Jason, author.
 1-to-1 at home : a parent's guide to school-issued laptops and tablets / Jason Brand. — Paperback edition.
     pages cm
 Includes bibliographical references.
 ISBN 978-1-56484-331-9
 1. Education—Data processing. 2. Educational technology. 3. Laptop computers. 4. Tablet computers. 5. Education—Parent participation. I. Title. II. Title: One-to-one at home.
 LB1028.43.B73 2013
 371.33'4—dc23

2013007362

First Edition
ISBN: 978-1-56484-331-9 (paperback)
Printed in the United States of America

Cover Art: © iStockphoto.com/CostinT, © iStockphoto.com/PixelEmbargo
Inside Photographs: p. iv, Deborah Robison; p. 5, © ThinkStock.com/BananaStock; p. 19, © iStockphoto.com/LordRunar; p. 65, © iStockphoto.com/nycshooter; p. 77, © Veer.com/Monkey Business Images
Comic Illustrations, pp. 67–75, Chase Cranor

ISTE® is a registered trademark of the International Society for Technology in Education.

About ISTE

The International Society for Technology in Education (ISTE) is the trusted source for professional development, knowledge generation, advocacy, and leadership for innovation. ISTE is the premier membership association for educators and education leaders engaged in improving teaching and learning by advancing the effective use of technology in PK–12 and teacher education.

Home to ISTE's annual conference and exposition and the widely adopted NETS, ISTE represents more than 100,000 professionals worldwide. We support our members with information, networking opportunities, and guidance as they face the challenge of transforming education. To find out more about these and other ISTE initiatives, visit our website at www.iste.org.

As part of our mission, ISTE Book Publishing works with experienced educators to develop and produce practical resources for classroom teachers, teacher educators, and technology leaders. Every manuscript we select for publication is carefully peer-reviewed and professionally edited. We value your feedback on this book and other ISTE products. Email us at books@iste.org.

International Society for Technology in Education
Washington, DC, Office:
    1710 Rhode Island Ave. NW, Suite 900, Washington, DC 20036-3132
Eugene, Oregon, Office:
    180 West 8th Ave., Suite 300, Eugene, OR 97401-2916
Order Desk: 1.800.336.5191
Order Fax: 1.541.302.3778
Customer Service: orders@iste.org
Book Publishing: books@iste.org
Book Sales and Marketing: booksmarketing@iste.org
Web: www.iste.org

About the Author

Jason Brand, LCSW, is a psychotherapist in the San Francisco Bay Area. He also has a master of arts degree in critical studies with an emphasis in new media. He provides support to families and educators as they discover that digital technologies are transforming their lives in unforeseen ways.

Part of Brand's work takes place in schools and with organizations where he leads workshops about safety, trust, awareness, and respect in the digital age. He has worked closely with many school communities that have started 1-to-1 laptop and tablet programs and as director of a program for children that encourages creative projects through the use of new technologies. In his private practice, he counsels families with children and adolescents.

Dedication

To Jen, Talia, and Minna

Acknowledgments

It is a great pleasure to acknowledge the people who have helped me in the process of writing this guidebook.

My family provides me with steady support that makes projects like this one possible. I feel very fortunate to have parents who are generous with their love, time, energy, and willingness to share their knowledge and experience. My sister, Rachel, has helped me in so many ways, big and small, and I love her dearly. Steve, my future brother-in-law, I thank for his help in thinking through the digital plan and being such a wonderful addition to the family. My daughters, Talia and Minna, I love and thank for being my best teachers. And, to my wife, Jen, who has an amazing ability to keep an eye out for all of the details while staying connected to my heart and soul, I want to express my love and endless thanks.

I leaned on the help of our wonderful community to help me throughout this process. A special thank you to my mentor, Sheri Glucoft Wong, who has given me so much guidance over the years. And special thanks to Richard Topel and Tamara Lerner for their constant support and love.

Many thanks to Gene Seltzer and Jack Litewka for their generous guidance and to Courtney Burkholder at ISTE for her enthusiastic approach to publishing and enthusiasm for the project.

To the following individuals, in no particular order, I express my gratitude: the Bakal family, Ozzie "Heart-throb never" Brand, Ty Alper, Ned Smock, Jon Givner, Rona Renner, Pay Rose, Linda Pazdierk, Ali Lawrence, Naomi Lucks, Ariela Wilcox, Stefan Cohen, Daniel Cukierman, Jane Wattenberg, "Uncle" Steve Brier, Jane Kagon, Harriet Kimble Wrye, Susan Shaffer, Bonnie Nishihara, Douglas Gostlin, Jared Finklestein, the Marin Parents Group.

Finally, to all the families and schools I have had the opportunity to work with who inspired this guidebook, I extend my wholehearted thanks.

Contents

Foreword ix
Preface xi

Introduction 1

Chapter 1
Get Ready! *Before* the 1-to-1 Device Comes Home 5
    Understand the Vision of 1-to-1 Learning 6
    Get Clear on the School's Responsibilities and the Family's Responsibilities 9
    Sign the 1-to-1 Child and Parent Agreement 16

Chapter 2
Get Set! Decisions about Specific Issues 19
    Parental Control, Filtering, and Monitoring Software 20
    Downloading Media 27
    Video Sites 32
    Social Networks 37
    Video Games 43
    Video, Voice, and Text Chatting 51
    Ergonomics and Sleep 56

Chapter 3
Go! Guidelines for the Five Biggest Challenges 65
    Who Takes Responsibility for the 1-to-1 Device? 66
    What Do Families Need to Understand about the 1-to-1 Environment? .. 69
    How Do Families Set Limits on a Boundary-Blurring Device? 71
    What's the Right Amount of Privacy? 72
    How Much Screen Time Is the Right Amount? 75

Chapter 4
Stop! Reset If Something Goes Wrong 77
    Typical Issues 78
    Issues Requiring Adult Attention 79
    Red Flags 81
    Hitting the Reset Button 81

Conclusion 85

Appendix A: Forms and Checklists 87
    Form A.1: School and Parent Guidelines and Responsibilities
    for the 1-to-1 Device 89
    Form A.2: Child Guidelines and Responsibilities Agreement
    for the 1-to-1 Device 92
    Form A.3: 1-to-1 Family Agreement 95
    Form A.4: Record for the 1-to-1 Device 100

Appendix B: Resources 101
    General Background Resources 101
    Resources for Specific Issues 103

Foreword

Way too much fear has been imposed on the public conversation about children and technology in the news media and policy circles. Because we tend to fear what we do not fully understand, all the fear-based messages have colored, if not hampered, parents' own learning about the tech part of parenting. What can really help parents are lots of two-way communication (especially with their kids and also with everyone involved in their kids' online experiences) plus solid information based on research and real-life experiences. *1-to-1 at Home* encourages the former and provides the latter.

The media and technologies children love and use avidly every day at home need to be available in school—not just for greater engagement in the classroom (though that is likely to happen), but also so children can learn how to function effectively in the workplaces and communities of a digital age. They need the opportunities to practice the citizenship and literacies of digital environments as part of their K–12 education: they need schools outfitted with digital media and technologies.

1-to-1 laptop and tablet programs get us closer to that ideal. Essentially, these programs collapse the imaginary "firewalls" between what happens at school and what happens at home *and* between what happens online and what happens offline. In our highly interactive, increasingly mobile, digital media environment, learning, social life, research, entertainment, and more happen everywhere and any time.

An imaginary firewall was built between home and school since the advent of social media in the middle of the last decade, as our uses of social media have dissolved any distinctions we might've thought there were between our online and offline lives. There are no firewalls, especially for our children. We know that kids make little distinction between online and offline in their social lives. And research shows us that all kinds of learning—sometimes the formal kind, sometimes the informal kind—are occurring in online communities, games, and other digital media. So why put up artificial walls in our children's learning experiences? Fortunately, 1-to-1 programs are bringing schools into the age of all-the-time, anywhere learning, which our children have been embracing for some time on their own. Now that

Foreword

more educators are using 1-to-1 programs, learning at school is becoming more relevant to students. And fortunately, this book is here to help digital nonnatives in schools and families let go of viewpoints and misconceptions that may stand in the way of all-the-time, anywhere learning.

With the help of *1-to-1 at Home*, we can get on with supporting wise, clear-eyed use of digital media and technology at home and at school.

Anne Collier
Executive Director Net Family News, Inc.
Co-director ConnectSafely.org

Preface

I believe we cannot address online concerns with a fear-based approach. Scaring kids away from new technologies is not a viable option—it is not realistic, and it sends the wrong message. 1-to-1 programs are just one example of how new technologies are transforming the ways we learn and work. Acknowledging this reality and teaching kids to use these tools responsibly is the priority. In my work and in *1-to-1 at Home*, I have striven to offer an approach that helps families work together to connect their unique values with their child's passions.

I wrote this guidebook after working closely with many school communities that have started 1-to-1 laptop and 1-to-1 tablet programs. *1-to-1 at Home* recognizes what I heard repeated by many parents: "1-to-1 programs are a game changer."

As I did the research for this book, I spoke with many technology directors, teachers, school counselors, and administrators. All of these educators were struggling with a similar challenge: they were trying to figure out how to better support their students' parents. They saw how their 1-to-1 programs were blurring the boundaries between home and school and how the changes brought about by these programs were causing unintended consequences for families.

Repeatedly, I heard about "the vocal minority" (parents who were unhappy with the schools' 1-to-1 programs). These parents often led schools to seek my help. They felt that the 1-to-1 device took an already complicated area—setting rules and limits around technology use—and made it almost impossible to manage. The schools were looking to support these parents by finding ways to make their 1-to-1 learning environment fit more comfortably into families' rules and values.

My support came in the form of parent education evenings and individual consultations with parents and administrators. What I found through these interventions was a unique set of challenges in 1-to-1 schools. Challenges were often expressed by only a small minority of parents, but when I was able to help them express their concerns openly, I learned that dealings between parents and children related to the schools' 1-to-1 programs were actually complicated for all families. I also found that when schools clearly explained the challenges and benefits of 1-to-1 learning to parents and provided them with suggested guidelines to follow within a supportive home structure, the best interests of parents, students, and, ultimately, entire school communities were served.

This guidebook combines my work as a therapist who specializes in helping families to navigate in an increasingly digital world with the techniques and materials that I developed for 1-to-1 schools. In this book, parents will find practical information to help them organize the details of being responsible for the 1-to-1 device, learn best practices from diverse school communities, and understand ways families can approach the digital dilemmas that come up when the 1-to-1 device comes home.

If 1-to-1 programs are going to live up to their promise of revolutionizing education, parents need to be involved. I believe that once this happens, parents will have increasing opportunities to become supportive, informative resources as schools educate their children.

I offer this guidebook to provide parents and educators with ways to address the needs of the home side of 1-to-1 programs. In my work with 1-to-1 schools, it became clear to me that families needed additional resources to help them understand how to adapt to the changes that laptops and tablets create at home. This book illustrates how parents and educators can get along better with these young learners while helping them to become more responsible technology users.

1-to-1 programs are relatively new. This means that schools are responsible for educating parents to understand the positive potential benefits that their children will gain and for providing parents with the support they need to understand that 1-to-1 programs create educational assets, not liabilities. I am happy to offer this guidebook of resources as steps toward that future and to address current challenges families face. I look forward to hearing how educators utilize this book and hope that it inspires them to build new bridges between homes and schools.

Jason Brand, LCSW
Jason@jasonbrand.com
www.jasonbrand.com

Introduction

The days of a child sitting with an open textbook, receiving information from the teacher at the front of a classroom are numbered. Over the next 10 years, we will see an inevitable change in education as schools embrace the digital classroom.

Schools at the forefront of this change are adopting 1-to-1 programs. These programs provide each student with a laptop or tablet that is used at school and at home. The goal is to educate a generation of students born into a digital culture and emerging into a world that requires a new set of skills.

This is a big transition, and schools are still in the process of understanding how "digital assistants," such as laptops and tablets, fit into the learning environment. Schools, however, are not acting in a vacuum. For this transition to be truly successful, each child's whole world needs to be considered. This requires everyone responsible for young people to be involved. Families—along with the home environment—are too often missing from this equation.

Getting families on board with 1-to-1 learning programs requires preparation, including educators knowing how to conduct appropriate conversations and giving parents some support if something goes awry. Parents who are resistant to their children having laptops or tablets need to understand why schools are adopting these programs and find ways to remain true to their values while embracing the change. This practical, hands-on guidebook is written to support the 1-to-1 program at home.

How is the 1-to-1 device (a laptop or tablet) different from all the other gadgets, gizmos, and game players that your family might already own?

- It comes from school.
- It impacts the amount of screen time—the time kids are engaged with digital technologies.
- It adds new responsibilities to home life.
- It blurs the distinction between tool and toy: it's harder to know if kids are studying, playing, or socializing.
- It changes how parents establish rules and set limits.

- It asks parents to respect school rules around the acceptable use of technology.
- It asks parents to respect school values about the role technology should play in a child's life.
- Most critically, it may require parents to take a new approach to their parenting as well as to the technology.

For parents, managing the gadgets, gizmos, and game players that their kids already own is often challenge enough. Many parents find that the 1-to-1 device provided at school further disrupts an area where there are already conflicts between parents and children. The good news is that these challenges can also become strengths, because the 1-to-1 device is not just about games and entertainment—it is also about school and education. This requires families to get to the heart of the matter. With proper support and good information, parents can understand new technologies, accepting the central role they increasingly play in our and our children's lives while making room for rules and limits that are in line with the family's unique values.

This guidebook is written from the perspective of a family therapist who has the skills and training to help families get to the heart of complicated matters. Two key ingredients in doing this successfully are parents having the language and the techniques to keep conversations on track with the useful perspectives of other adults who have addressed similar challenges.

This book contains many examples of language that parents can use to clearly communicate guidelines and rules in ways that kids are likely to listen to and respond to favorably. The language that this guidebook provides has been tested in consultations and with groups of parents who were struggling to set fair guidelines for their children's use of laptops or tablets at home. The *Get Set* section (Chapter 2) includes quotes from parents and educators about common areas where families struggle with the 1-to-1 device's role. The quotes were gathered in dozens of parent and teacher education workshops and through online surveys.

This guidebook takes the familiar approaches of learning a new skill or sport: *Get ready... Get set... Go...*, and, in Chapter 4, *Stop* (and reset if something goes wrong). It starts by preparing parents to have a 1-to-1 learning device in their home that their children are required by their teachers to use for homework, research, and class projects. The material herein gets them set and on the go by understanding the areas where problems often arise and learning the most effective attitudes and methods for dealing with these complex issues. Parents will also learn how to stop reacting and how to start reconsidering or revising their actions when something goes wrong.

1-to-1 at Home is also designed to be a practical companion. It provides places to keep track of the details (serial number, insurance information, technical support contact information, etc.) that parents will want to have organized and at their fingertips.

When parents are prepared, they can partner with schools to embrace the 1-to-1 program, understanding that they can help their children explore the beneficial, exciting possibilities of learning in a digital environment.

A Note to Parents

You need additional, specific support to manage the impact that your child's 1-to-1 device has on family life. This guidebook provides that support by addressing the home side of 1-to-1 programs. It helps you to be aware of shifts in 21st-century learning and to take realistic approaches to integrating a school-issued laptop or tablet into your family thoughtfully and responsibly.

A Note to Educators

Technology directors, teachers, school counselors, and administrators—you are often faced with figuring out how to better support parents. This guidebook can be used by educators of new or established 1-to-1 school communities in your efforts to build bridges with the parents of the children you serve.

Chapter 1

Get Ready!
Before the 1-to-1 Device Comes Home

Many parents take a wait-and-see approach to 1-to-1 devices. They trust that the school has thought through any issues that might come up, or they figure that the laptop or tablet will be similar to any other Internet-connected gadget, gizmo, or game player that their child already has.

Chapter 1   Get Ready!   *Before* the 1-to-1 Device Comes Home

Over and over again, parents have told me that they were caught off guard by the impact of their child's 1-to-1 device. This is a big transition, and schools are still in the process of understanding how "digital assistants" fit into the learning environment. Equally important is the need to think through the home side of these powerful tools/toys. The 1-to-1 device is different from other computers and technological devices in the home; it's meant to serve several different functions. Thus, *before* students bring their 1-to-1 device home, parents must understand exactly how and why the device is being used. Just as laptops or tablets change the way kids learn at school, these devices will also change the culture of your family. In other words, the presence of these interactive devices in your home will call for you as parents and your children to find some new ways of communicating and agreeing on responsibilities.

This section is designed to get your family prepared for a 1-to-1 program. Even if your family is already part of a 1-to-1 program and the 1-to-1 device is already brought home from school and stays over every weekend, it's not too late to go back and get everyone on the same page.

The objectives for this chapter are to accomplish the following:

- Understand the vision of 1-to-1 learning.
- Get clear on the school's responsibilities and the family's responsibilities.
- Sign the 1-to-1 parent, child, and family agreements.

After you and your child have achieved these objectives, you will understand how to set appropriate boundaries for using the device at home that fit with your family's values and priorities, including your and your child's responsibilities!

Understand the Vision of 1-to-1 Learning

Why would a school give a student a laptop or tablet that is a tool for learning as well as a toy for playing games and socializing? Why would many schools want to blur the line between schools' responsibilities and families' responsibilities? Answering these questions is an important part of making the 1-to-1 program work for all members of your family.

In the following box, Scott McLeod, a leading thinker in technology in education, explains why schools are adopting 1-to-1 programs and his vision of 21st-century learning.

Box 1.1 A Message from Scott McLeod

It's Not a Paper-and-Pencil World Anymore

Let's start with the recognition that digital technologies are transforming EVERYTHING.

This fact is unsettling to many parents and educators.

Why?

Simply stated, digital technologies are disruptive. They allow everyone to do work that is more powerful and complex with greater creative capability. For instance, the same technologies that allow us to have a voice, to find each other, and to work together have disrupted our sense of geographic boundaries and time barriers. As a result, we are seeing (to our dismay) that offshoring and outsourcing allow everyone, everywhere to compete with each other and with us. In addition to replacing jobs here with people overseas, jobs also are being destroyed by software. If the Industrial Revolution was about replacing humans' physical labor with machines, the Information Revolution often is about replacing humans' cognitive labor with computers. In short, these new tools are radically transforming every single information-oriented segment of our economy. As information institutions, schools will not be immune.

Schools that adopt 1-to-1 programs are taking a proactive stance to this disruption by providing students with the skills and attitudes necessary to take advantage of the opportunities that digital technologies provide.

Digital technologies allow for dramatic impacts on learning. For example, students and educators now have access to all of the information in their textbooks—and an incredible wealth of primary documents—for free. They have access to robust, low-cost or no-cost multimedia and interactive learning resources—texts, images, audio, video, games, simulations—that can supplement, extend, or even replace what is being taught in their classrooms. Via collaborative Internet-based tools, they can learn from and with students and teachers in other states or countries. They also can quickly and easily connect with authors, artists, business professionals, entrepreneurs, physicians, craftsmen, professors, and other experts.

Continued

Box 1.1 A Message from Scott McLeod *Continued*

> Students and teachers now can more authentically replicate (and actually do) real-world work through the use of the same tools and resources used by engineers, designers, scientists, accountants, and a multitude of other professionals and artisans. Students can share their own knowledge, skills, and expertise with people all over the world. They can find or form communities of interest around topics for which they are passionate, and they can be active (and valued) contributors to the world's information commons, both individually and collaboratively with others.
>
> Essentially, our students and teachers now have the ability to learn about whatever they want, from whomever they want, whenever and wherever they want, and they also can contribute to this learning environment for the benefit of others.
>
> Workers in the real world (i.e., outside of school) use computers to do their work. Can educators really claim to be relevant to students and society while simultaneously ignoring the technological transformations that surround them? It's a digital, global world out there. Schools that are serious about preparing their graduates for a technology-suffused information society do everything they can to put a robust digital learning device into every student's hands instead of pretending that we live in a pencil, notebook paper, and ring binder world.
>
> Scott McLeod, JD, PhD
> Associate Professor and Founding Director of CASTLE
> University of Kentucky

For more information on Scott McLeod's work and on the Center for the Advanced Study of Technology Leadership in Education, CASTLE, see http://leadership.uky.edu/centers-services/castle.

Get Clear on the School's Responsibilities and the Family's Responsibilities

As the 1-to-1 device travels from home to school and back again, guidelines and responsibilities can be confusing for parents and children. Each school provides different levels of support to prepare families for a 1-to-1 program. Filling out the blank versions of Figure 1.1 and Figure 1.2 (Forms A.1 and A.2, found in Appendix A at the end of this book) will help you to get clear on some common areas where guidelines and responsibilities need to be established. Ideally, schools will provide information for these forms at a parent education evening. If your school does not offer a special meeting to review information about the 1-to-1 device, set up a time to talk to the teacher or school administrator in charge of the 1-to-1 program so that you can take home copies of the school's guidelines and list of responsibilities for parents and children.

Note that in the sample based on Form A.1 (Figure 1.1), some responsibilities might be assumed by the school, some by the parent/s, and some by both family and school. Form A.1, School and Parent Guidelines and Responsibilities, is divided into three parts:

- Physical care and maintenance of the equipment
- Student and family social and emotional support
- Specific issues and challenges

Form A.2, Child Guidelines and Responsibilities Agreement, has three divisions similar to those in Form A.1:

- Physical care and maintenance of the equipment
- Student social and emotional support
- Specific issues and challenges

Additional cells are provided in case you wish to add further responsibilities to Form A.1 or further agreements to Form A.2.

Chapter 1   Get Ready!   *Before* the 1-to-1 Device Comes Home

Figure 1.1 Sample of Completed Form A.1: *School and Parent Guidelines and Responsibilities for the 1-to-1 Device*

School and Parent Guidelines and Responsibilities

Physical Care and Maintenance of the Equipment

School	Parent	Responsibility	Notes
✓		Provide an acceptable use policy (AUP) for taking care of the equipment.	Handed out with laptop; students already signed.
✓		Provide a protective case for the equipment.	
	✓	Provide a policy for adding additional software or hardware.	No official policy but need to check with tech person before adding software/hardware.
✓		Provide a policy on decorating the 1-to-1 device.	No decorating the 1-to-1 device!
	✓	Provide a policy on charging the 1-to-1 device to ensure that it will have a full battery during the school day.	
✓		Provide tips to encourage students to bring a fully charged 1-to-1 device to school each day.	School suggests buying an extra charger that is always plugged into the same outlet in our home.
✓		Provide information and policies about backing up student work.	Most work saved in the cloud; email tech director with specific questions.

Figure 1.1 Sample of Completed Form A.1 *Continued*

Student and Family Social and Emotional Support

School	Parent	Responsibility	Notes
✓		Provide an acceptable use policy (AUP) that covers social behavior and the 1-to-1 device.	Signed by students before laptops were handed out. Go over at home.
✓		Provide students with opportunities to learn about Internet safety and digital citizenship.	Student assembly on October 15. Ongoing conversation in Health and Life Skills class.
✓		Provide a parent education evening about social and emotional issues and the 1-to-1 device.	Date & Time: October 15, 7–8:30pm
	✓	Provide ongoing opportunities for a dialogue between parents and the school to discuss the impacts of the 1-to-1 device on home life.	Email PTA president to join group that will meet monthly.
	✓	Provide a policy about other people (siblings, friends, parents) using the equipment.	We need to do this!
✓		Provide a policy about how the laptop/tablet will be used during school breaks (lunch, recess, etc.).	1-to-1 device only allowed in designated area where teacher is present.

Continued

Chapter 1 Get Ready! *Before* the 1-to-1 Device Comes Home

Figure 1.1 Sample of Completed Form A.1 *Continued*

Specific Issues and Challenges

School	Parent	Responsibility	Notes
✓	✓	Provide parental control, filtering, and/or monitoring software.	We can use our own, but school encourages using software that came with 1-to-1 device.
	✓	Provide information about when the 1-to-1 device can be used (e.g., at night after bedtime, on weekends).	We need to go over this at home!
✓	✓	Provide information and guidelines about how much time a student should spend using the 1-to-1 device per school day and on weekends for school-related projects.	School encourages us to talk with our child. Teachers will let us know about school-related projects requiring additional at-home time on the device.
✓	✓	Provide guidelines about what types of videos, music, and text constitute explicit content (i.e., sexual, violent, profane) and rules about storing or viewing this content on the 1-to-1 device.	Covered in AUP but should match with our home values.
✓	✓	Provide guidelines about chatting (video or text) and the 1-to-1 device.	Covered in AUP but should match with our home values.
	✓	Provide guidelines about playing video games on the 1-to-1 device.	This is up to parents, but school allows no games with explicit content/rated M (mature) by ESRB (Entertainment Software Rating Board; see www.esrb.org).
	✓	Provide guidelines about using social network sites on the 1-to-1 device.	Facebook is not allowed on the 1-to-1 device, but up to parents about other social networks.
	✓	Provide information about ergonomics and avoiding repetitive stress injuries.	Up to parents.

Once a clearer sense of parent and school responsibilities are in place, you can help your child understand and agree to take on the responsibilities described in Form A.2. This agreement form should be filled out at home with your child. Your child writes his/her initials beside each item as it is mutually agreed upon with the parent/s. Parents are encouraged to write their initials beside each item. Ideally both parents will participate in the discussion. Parents might add their initials to each item to indicate their commitment to the agreement.

Figure 1.2 Sample of Completed Form A.2: *Child Guidelines and Responsibilities Agreement for the 1-to-1 Device*

Child Guidelines and Responsibilities Agreement

Physical Care and Maintenance of the Equipment

Child (initials)	Agreement	Notes (details, date, parent initials)
SJ	Understands and agrees to follow acceptable use policy on taking care of the equipment.	Went over school agreement at home on Sept. 20. DJ MJ
SJ	Understands and agrees to follow policy on adding additional software or hardware.	Talk to school about adding dictation program. Went over policy at home on Sept. 20. DJ MJ
SJ	Understands and agrees to follow policy on decorating the 1-to-1 device.	Went over policy at home Sept. 20. DJ MJ
SJ	Understands and agrees to follow policy on charging the 1-to-1 device to ensure that it will have a full battery during the school day.	Set up central place in the kitchen to charge the 1-to-1 device. Agreed that this is one of SJ's chores. Went over policy at home Sept. 20. DJ MJ
SJ	Understands and agrees to follow policies on backing up student work.	SJ showed us how he backs up schoolwork using the Internet. Agreed this is his responsibility. Went over at home on Sept. 20. DJ MJ

Continued

Figure 1.2 Sample of Completed Form A.2   *Continued*

\multicolumn{3}{l}{*Student Social and Emotional Support*}
Child	Agreement	Notes
SJ	Understands and agrees to follow acceptable use policy that covers social behavior and the 1-to-1 device.	On September 20th and 24th we talked about the need to make good social choices on the 1-to-1 device and signed off on the items below. *DJ MJ*
SJ	Understands and agrees to follow policy on other people (siblings, friends, parents) not being allowed to use the equipment.	*Talked about siblings and friends not being allowed to use the 1-to-1 device. Went over at home on Sept. 20.* **DJ MJ**
SJ	Understands and agrees to follow policy on how the laptop/tablet will be used during school breaks (lunch, recess, etc.)	*SJ understands school policy on this; teacher explained policy at school on day 1-to-1 device was handed out. Agreed with us not to spend too many lunches on the device. We discussed this at home on Sept. 24.* **DJ MJ**

Figure 1.2 Sample of Completed Form A.2 *Continued*

\multicolumn{3}{l}{*Specific Issues and Challenges*}
Child	Agreement	Notes
SJ	Understands and agrees to how parental control, filtering, and/or monitoring software will be used.	On Sept. 24, we discussed these items with SJ and agreed on the ones that apply to our family. DJ MJ
SJ	Understands and agrees to times when the 1-to-1 device can be used (such as at night after bedtime, on weekends).	Will leave the 1-to-1 device in the kitchen after 9:30 p.m. Went over this at home on Sept. 24. DJ MJ
SJ	Understands and agrees to follow school guidelines on how much time a student should spend using the 1-to-1 device per school day and on weekends for school-related projects.	SJ needs to check in with his teachers to get this one checked off. He's agreed to give us this information by Sept. 26. DJ MJ
SJ	Agrees to follow school guidelines on what videos, music, and text constitute explicit content and to follow rules about storing or viewing this content on the 1-to-1 device.	We set up parental controls on iTunes together with SJ. He agreed to keep any music with questionable lyrics off the 1-to-1 device. He agreed to keep videos and text with explicit content off the device per ESRB guidelines. Went over at home on Sept. 24. DJ MJ
SJ	Agrees to guidelines on chatting (video or text) and the 1-to-1 device.	Talked about chatting only with classmates on 1-to-1 device or getting a parent's permission to chat with people outside school. Went over at home on Sept. 24. DJ MJ

Continued

Figure 1.2 Sample of Completed Form A.2   *Continued*

SJ	Agrees to guidelines on playing video games on the 1-to-1 device.	Will not play video games on the 1-to-1 device. SJ understands he may use the home personal computer per our family's agreement to play video games. Went over at home on Sept. 24. **DJ MJ**
SJ	Agrees to guidelines on using social network sites on the 1-to-1 device.	Will not use social network sites on 1-to-1 device. Will use Facebook only on home personal computer. Went over at home on Sept. 24. **DJ MJ**
SJ	Understands and agrees to follow guidelines on ergonomics and avoiding repetitive stress injuries.	Bought special mouse and keyboard for SJ's 1-to-1 device. Went over at home on Sept. 24. **DJ MJ**

Sign the 1-to-1 Child and Parent Agreement

A practical way to get everyone on the same page when it comes to the 1-to-1 program is to sit down together and fill out a family agreement. The 1-to-1 Child and Parent Agreement, Form A.3, appears in the appendix at the end of this book. *It is best to sit down with your child and fill out the agreement after reviewing the contents of this guidebook.*

This agreement is written mainly for kids who are in middle school and high school, but in many areas it could be used with mature elementary school children. The agreement keeps the whole family in mind and is specific to the 1-to-1 program. With this agreement in place, you will have opened a dialogue not only about rules and guidelines, but also will have made it clear that everyone has a role in making the 1-to-1 program work in your family.

Benefits of the Family Agreement

Child safety. Many families use formal or informal agreements to ensure that kids are kept safe when they are at home or when their parents are responsible for them at night and on weekends. A list of rules and guidelines are spelled out, confusing areas are clarified, and kids are provided with a sense of the boundaries between acceptable and unacceptable behaviors. Talking about the safe use of the 1-to-1 device is one of the benefits of this agreement.

Trust. Another benefit of this agreement is taking time to discuss the concept of trust when it comes to the 1-to-1 device. The device is going to be used in many settings for many different purposes, and it will be present both at home and at school. This is a big responsibility—one that parents cannot expect to monitor at all times; therefore, parents and children need to trust each other. This agreement can be a terrific opportunity for families to develop more trusting relationships in various area of their lives together—not only those that are affected by the device.

Awareness. This agreement also builds awareness for children. Many of the mistakes that kids make online happen when there is a lack of awareness about how their actions on a 1-to-1 device produce a unique set of consequences.

Parental involvement. This agreement provides parents with a chance to pause and to explain the bigger picture about how the 1-to-1 program connects a child's whole world. Parents can also use this as an opportunity for gaining greater awareness of their child's world. Parents can build credibility and be a positive influence by actively participating in the parent part of this agreement.

Respect. Finally, this agreement can benefit your family through fostering a sense of mutual respect. Kids want respect from their peers, parents, and teachers. Parents want to feel a sense of respect from their children. This agreement helps families describe how making positive choices while using the 1-to-1 device can help families build self- and mutual respect.

After spending some time reviewing the agreement, sign it, shake on it, and keep it where it will not be covered up by other papers. You might consider placing it in a folder with plastic page covers. It could be kept near the 1-to-1 device's charger so everyone knows where to find it.

Chapter 2

Get Set!

Decisions about Specific Issues

There are several areas where problems are likely to arise with the 1-to-1 device. In this chapter, we'll explore these areas and provide checklists and online resources for specific issues.

| Chapter 2 | Get Set! Decisions about Specific Issues |

1-to-1 programs have been around long enough to pinpoint areas where parents struggle with setting limits and clarifying acceptable use. In some families, the 1-to-1 device disrupts already existing rules; in others, the 1-to-1 device grants kids access to applications that parents had not previously allowed. And, in some families, discussions about how the device is to be used at home make previously existing concerns or areas of disagreement that had nothing to do with a 1-to-1 device more pronounced. This chapter is written to give you information about these specific areas and to help everyone come together around a common set of guidelines.

The objectives of this chapter are to understand how to navigate issues that come up for 1-to-1 families and to clarify home and school rules.

Topics we'll discuss include

- Parental control, filtering, and monitoring software
- Downloading media
- Video sites
- Social networks
- Video games
- Video, voice, and text chatting

Parental Control, Filtering, and Monitoring Software

What is parental control software? There are many variations of parental control software; these tools can be installed (or come included with) almost any device that connects to the Internet. All the variations of parental control software share a common goal, which is to provide parents with greater control over their child's online behaviors. Filtering software generally means that words, phrases, and/or sites deemed inappropriate are blocked from showing up on a network or a particular computer. Monitoring software usually looks at the content that kids are uploading and downloading and provides a report to parents. Parental control software can also act to limit the amount of time kids spend on a particular site, on the Internet itself, and/or on video games. Many types of parental control software include the ability to do all three of these tasks—monitoring, filtering, and setting time limits.

Parents Speak

Parental control software tends to bring out strong feelings in parents. Parents who use it often report that they find it invaluable and see the decision to install it as obvious as having a lock on the front door of their home. Those who do not use it often say that they think of it as a form of snooping and feel it sends the wrong message about the role technology should play in their family's life. A third group of parents have tried using the software but became frustrated with the settings or keeping the software up to date and have given up on making it work for their family; if they could find a more user-friendly parental control software, they would be open to trying it again.

> **Parents and Educators Speak**
>
> The quotations in this chapter are from parents and educators who participated in numerous parent and teacher education workshops and in online surveys.

Ideally, when a child receives a 1-to-1 device, parents should take the opportunity to consider how monitoring and filtering software could be used with the device. Parents need to understand the school's approach to monitoring and filtering both at home and at school. Here are examples of different parents' perspectives on filtering and monitoring software, along with how these families can use the 1-to-1 device as an opportunity to make a thoughtful decision about parental control software:

> We use filtering software on all of the computers in our home, including the 1-to-1 device. We think of it like giving our son a map of where he can and can't go online. There is so much freedom online, and I like the idea of us having set some clear boundaries. On the 1-to-1 device, it seemed even more important to have a filter because the school is involved.
>
> Jerry, parent of a fifth grader

For parents who already use parental control software, the 1-to-1 device provides a point of comparison to their current filtering and monitoring strategy. For many families, the parental control software being used at home does not match with their child's age and level of maturity or is better suited for an older or younger sibling. Try to match the filtering level specifically to your child's maturity level.

Chapter 2 Get Set! Decisions about Specific Issues

> At our school we had a parent night where we learned about using parental controls on the iPad. It was one of the really good parts about getting the tablet because it forced us to sit down and really think about what we would want out of parental control software. We always thought it was too complicated, but it turns out that it's not that difficult. In the end, we decided to only use it on the least restrictive settings, but it's good to know it's there in case something goes wrong.
>
> Sharon, parent of a tenth grader

Sharon's quote highlights the importance of good support from the school. With the school's help, parents have an opportunity to learn more about the 1-to-1 device and the capabilities of filtering and monitoring software. Even if parents choose not to use parental control software, they have learned it might be a useful tool in the future. Thus, they view the software as an available resource to be used if their children need additional limits.

> [Before the 1-to-1 program] we started out using filtering software, but it got complicated when our [older] kids started writing research papers and it kept blocking sites that they needed. We would let them log into our parent account, which was not restricted, and then eventually we all got a little lazy and started letting our younger [seventh-grade] daughter use the nonrestricted account. Now we are using filtering software again because we have technical support from the school.
>
> Jonathan, parent of a seventh grader

Families who had given up on filtering and monitoring software because of technical difficulties now have the school's support to help them make the software work.

Educators Speak

At home, it is ultimately up to you to make sure that your child is using the 1-to-1 device responsibly. Some schools will be flexible in working with parents who want to use their own filtering or monitoring software on the 1-to-1 device. Parents also have to be open to the school's advice and the resources that schools offer. Filtering and monitoring the 1-to-1 device does not necessarily require software; parents can stay engaged with what their children are doing on 1-to-1 devices in a number of nontechnical ways.

Here are some thoughts from teachers and school administrators about ways that parents can stay engaged with what their kids are up to.

> I think parental controls should be used as a last resort. It is better if parents and their child can develop a trusting relationship in regard to laptop use. This trusting relationship is important in all domains of parenting, whether it be laptop use, giving your child the independence to go out with friends, complete homework, etc. If you cannot have trust with your child in regard to the laptop, I believe this spills into all other areas of parenting.
>
> Douglas, school counselor in Berkeley, California

With all of the concerns about raising a child who has access to powerful digital tools, it can be easy to forget the obvious importance of a strong relationship. Parental control software can never replace building a trusting and respectful relationship with your child.

> Our computers currently have a filtering system that is active both at home and school. I encourage parents to have students use laptops in an open area and not allow them to be used in their bedrooms. I encourage parents to look over their students' laptops from time to time. A parent has every right to ask what their child is doing and to take the computer away. I encourage parents to talk openly with their child about responsible use of technology.
>
> Cari, principal in Conrad, Iowa

Chapter 2 Get Set! Decisions about Specific Issues

With a 1-to-1 program, parents have the difficult task of learning about a new technology along with their child, while maintaining their role as parent. This requires parents to learn some new strategies, but it is still necessary to keep familiar, tried-and-tested strategies in mind. It is important for parents to keep their ears and eyes alert for trouble and step in when something does not seem right.

> Be aware that in 1-to-1 programs where the device goes home, the school can no longer limit Internet interaction. It is, therefore, extremely important that parents have a constant, open dialogue with respect to off-campus Internet uses, as well as a clear set of family rules and guidelines for Internet use. Parents must also make periodic inspections of the device while it is at home—and this is the part that frightens most parents. They do not feel they know enough to properly police today's devices. But like other aspects of parenting, informing oneself becomes an essential practice that must not be eschewed for the sake of personal comfort. Policing—or a better term, good parenting—can be as simple as learning to check a device's browser history and the potential deletion of browser history.
>
> Thomas, iPad integration coordinator in Watsonville, California

If not knowing enough about how the 1-to-1 device works is keeping you from feeling like you can parent effectively, it is important to reach out for help. The school can often provide support. You can also ask for other parents' help or ask your child to demonstrate how he or she is using the 1-to-1 device. On page 26 you will find additional online resources.

Checklist 1

Parental Control, Filtering, and Monitoring Software

☐ Find out what options are available on the 1-to-1 device for parental control, filtering, and monitoring software.

☐ Decide if parental control, filtering, and/or monitoring software is right for your family.

If you use parental control, filtering, and/or monitoring software on the other Internet-connected devices in your home,

  ☐ Decide whether you want to use this same software on the 1-to-1 device.

  ☐ If you want to use the same software, find out if it is allowed by the school.

☐ If you decide to use parental control, filtering, and/or monitoring software, explain to your child how and when it will be used.

☐ Sit down with your child and fill out the 1-to-1 Child and Parent Agreement (Appendix A, Form A.3), discussed in Chapter 1.

The School's Policy

_____

_____

_____

_____

Our Family Policy

_____

_____

_____

_____

Chapter 2   Get Set!   Decisions about Specific Issues

Resources: Parental Control, Filtering, and Monitoring Software

Many parental control tools are included with your operating system or Internet service. Looking into the capabilities of these tools is a good place to start.

Google's Family Safety Center
> www.google.com/goodtoknow/familysafety
>> Google's Family Safety Center provides information about how families can safely use Google tools, including how to use SafeSearch, report inappropriate content, and share safety and privacy settings.

Apple's Parental Controls
> www.apple.com/findouthow/mac/#parentalcontrols
>> The Apple operating system provides parental control software.

Windows' Parental Controls
> http://windows.microsoft.com/en-US/windows-vista/Set-up-Parental-Controls
> http://windows.microsoft.com/en-US/windows7/Set-up-Parental-Controls
>> The Windows operating system provides parental control software.

Cable Companies' Parental Controls
> www.pointsmartclicksafe.org/parental-controls.html
>> If your cable company provides your Internet service, this site will lead you to resources that the cable companies provide for adding parental controls to the Internet-connected devices and computers in your home.

OpenDNS's Parental Controls
> www.opendns.com/home-solutions
>> OpenDNS provides a free home version that allows parents to filter content for all devices that connect to the home router.

Parenting Online Kids
> www.netfamilynews.org/the-trust-factor-in-parenting-online-kids (part one) &
> www.netfamilynews.org/parenting-or-digital-public-humiliation (part two)
>> This good, two-part article discusses why parents should be open with their children about the need for monitoring and filtering.

Downloading Media

What does "downloading media" entail? The term *downloading media* describes receiving music, video games, movies, or books from a remote system and copying the data as digital files that reside on the 1-to-1 device's hard drive. This is different from watching a video on a site like YouTube, where the file being watched is streamed and remains on YouTube's servers. Downloading media can either be legal or illegal, depending on how the digital files are obtained. Obtaining media from sites such as Apple's iTunes Store and Amazon.com's Amazon MP3 store is legal; these sites usually charge a fee for each download.

Parents Speak

Many parents are caught off guard by the fact that the 1-to-1 device can be used to download media. Your child's school will likely not limit access to the places where media can be purchased legally because these places can also be used for their wealth of educational resources. Parents who know a little bit about this ahead of time can avoid many problems, but learning a little too late can lead to frustration and conflict.

Chances are that your child will ask to download a favorite song, movie, or video game, and it will likely require a fee. If you are unfamiliar with how legal media download sites work, take the time to understand these sites along with your child. Also, take the time to discuss and set up rules and guidelines about how much money may be spent, the types of content that are acceptable, and where and when media can be used on the 1-to-1 device.

> We were completely caught off guard by the laptop's ability to download music, videos, and apps. Our daughter really got into music right around the same time she got the laptop. We had never allowed her to download music onto our home computer, and then all of a sudden there was a virtual record store in our living room. Of course, she wanted to buy everything, was spending hours browsing, and we really were not comfortable with some of the music she wanted to download. It's still an issue around our house. Had we known that this would be a part of her having the laptop from school, we could have been more prepared to talk about it from the beginning.
>
> Marci, parent of a seventh grader

Chapter 2   Get Set!   Decisions about Specific Issues

The challenge for families who feel overwhelmed by their children's downloading of media is how to avoid a power struggle, where parent rules and limits are on one side and a child's creative interests are on the other. Parents do not want to send the message that they are against the music, movies, games, and social networking sites that kids are passionate about. In these situations, it is often necessary to begin the conversation with a fresh start and for parents to understand something about their child's enthusiasm for these activities, many of which the parents haven't experienced. Once kids feel that they have been seen and heard by their parents, it is often easier to talk about sensible rules and limits.

> Once we figured out how to not have the iTunes store link to our credit card and gave our child a "music allowance" on his own iTunes account, everything was fine.
>
> Jane, parent of a sixth grader

It can be hard for parents to wrap their minds around the concept of buying or downloading media online. While a physical piece of media (compact disk, cassette tape, record, etc.) is not being exchanged, the concept is still the same. It is important for kids to understand the value of paying for media and supporting the artists, musicians, and designers who create media in any form. Jane's quote illustrates a sensible way to handle a child's enthusiasm for media and teach a lesson about sticking to a budget at the same time.

> We actually found listening to music on headphones on the iPad to be a real problem. Our kids are already so absorbed in all the technology, and it was frustrating to have our daughter completely cut off from what goes on in the house. Our rule is "No headphones in the house."
>
> Brett, parent of a ninth grader

The independent environment and autonomy that 1-to-1 learning allows can have an impact on other people; thus it is important to set limits that work for your family. For some families, listening to music while studying might not be a big deal, but for this particular family it made their daughter too removed from what was going on in the rest of the house. This is a good example of how negotiating issues like these successfully with your child is part of making the 1-to-1 program work at home.

Educators Speak

Two tasks for educators in a 1-to-1 school are to provide students with 21st-century tools and to help them understand how to use them thoughtfully. This requires schools to teach lessons that in earlier generations were taught at home. Downloading media raises a host of questions about the appropriateness of content, the morality of ownership, and the economics of exchange. These issues are now a part of the 1-to-1 learning environment. The following quotes from educators illustrate some of the ways that schools are helping students and their families navigate these issues.

> iTunes is currently the most popular purchasing portal. Parents should not allow their children access to an iTunes account password that is connected to a credit card. It is easy enough to have a device using an iTunes account with a password that only Mom and Dad know—this way, every purchase gets vetted by Mom and Dad before it's made; this includes music, games, movies, television, books, and all the media sold through iTunes. The purchases can go on the device, but the child needs the password to download anything new—it is through protecting the password that parents can ensure every purchase gets made with their direct approval. This includes free media—a password is still required. Another approach is to allow children to have their own iTunes accounts but not connect the account to a credit card. Gift cards with redemption codes can then be used to purchase media. However, this does not allow parents to observe what is being downloaded unless they remain vigilant throughout the redemption of the gift cards, and it does not allow parents to observe the downloading of free media.
>
> Thomas, iPad integration coordinator in Watsonville, California

There are practical things that informed parents can do to set limits when it comes to downloading media. Thomas's quote illustrates how practical strategies like having a password in place can act as an important way to check in with kids and keep parents informed about what media is being downloaded. Parents need to share these strategies within their school community—at meetings designated for this purpose and informally.

Chapter 2 Get Set! Decisions about Specific Issues

> We have iTunes available to students. We educate our students about copyright issues and share with them consequences to people who abuse the law.
>
> Cari, principal in Conrad, Iowa

An important 21st-century learning skill is to understand the value of media and information. One of the advantages of a 1-to-1 environment is that kids have greater opportunities to learn about the legal and moral issues that come up in a digital world, where media can be easily shared. Kids are growing up with the knowledge that there are always ways around paying for media. One of the most important moral lessons that schools and families need to provide for this generation of kids is "Just because I can get media for free with seemingly few consequences, does not mean that I should."

> We ask that restrictions are set so that explicit songs are blocked on student devices.
>
> Bonnie, director of technology, San Rafael, California

The line between what is explicit and what is edgy when it comes to media is often a difficult one to determine. It differs between generations and often requires parents to take the long view by remembering their own childhood music that their parents found distasteful. At the same time, the 1-to-1 device is also different from all of the devices that your family might own because it comes from the school. It is a good idea to be conservative with the digital media your child keeps on the 1-to-1 device. Discussing what is appropriate to store on the 1-to-1 device is a good conversation to have with your child. It develops critical thinking skills and can teach valuable lessons about best practices regarding where private media and information should be stored.

Get Set! Decisions about Specific Issues Chapter 2

Checklist 2

Downloading Media

☐ Find out if your child is allowed to download media (from portals such as iTunes) onto the 1-to-1 device.

☐ If your child is allowed to download media onto the 1-to-1 device, find out if there are school rules about the type of media that can be downloaded. (For example, are media with sexually or violently explicit lyrics allowed?)

☐ If your child is allowed to download media onto the 1-to-1 device, decide whether you will adopt home rules about the type of media that can be downloaded.

☐ If your child is allowed to download media onto the 1-to-1 device, find out the cost of downloading media and decide how media is going to be paid for. (For example, consider setting up a separate iTunes account for your child with an allowance.)

The School's Policy

_____
_____
_____
_____
_____

Our Family Policy

_____
_____
_____
_____
_____

Chapter 2 Get Set! Decisions about Specific Issues

Resources: Downloading Media

Common Sense Media Distinguishes Legal from Illegal Downloads
www.commonsensemedia.org/advice-for-parents/
illegal-downloads-when-sharing-becomes-stealing

> This good overview by Common Sense Media explains illegal downloading and advises parents on how to teach kids to respect copyright laws.

Apple's Parental Controls for iTunes' Content
http://support.apple.com/kb/ht1904

> Apple provides parental controls for iTunes that can help parents set limits on the kinds of content kids are allowed to download.

Apple Offers Parents an iTunes Allowance for Kids
http://support.apple.com/kb/HT2105

> Apple provides an "iTunes Allowance" feature for parents to provide kids with a set amount of credit for the iTunes store.

Setting Allowance and Parental Controls for iTunes on iPhones and iPads
www.quepublishing.com/articles/article.aspx?p=1917164

> This helpful article explains how to set up and use the allowance and parental control features in iTunes to work with an iPhone or an iPad.

Video Sites

What is a video site? Video sites like YouTube and Vimeo allow for sharing video files over the Internet. A vast collection of videos on these sites is shared by a wide range of users—from individuals to large media corporations. Users of these sites can share videos publicly or specify who can view their videos. These sites make money through advertisements and do not charge a membership fee to watch videos. To upload videos, a user must register with these sites. Registered users also have the option of adding ratings and comments to videos.

Parents Speak

Video sites highlight the great potential and challenges of learning in a 1-to-1 environment. On a video site, children can watch and re-watch the material from a math assignment and effectively learn at their own pace. They can also share information with a large audience and get valuable feedback from a diverse community. "Flipped" classrooms direct students to watch material from video sites at home on their 1-to-1 devices and then do their homework at school. In flipped classrooms, teachers further explain concepts from the video and encourage students to work through problems. This type of classroom means that parents no longer need to help kids with homework—or, as in many families, do their children's homework or make their kids' projects. Parents' biggest concerns are that their children may not get to their math assignments because of the 1-to-1 devices' limitless video distractions and the potential for their children to share inappropriate information (easily publishable for thousands to see) on social networking sites.

As the following comments from parents illustrate, video sites can be sources of frustration for parents. Many parents describe the challenges of getting kids to focus on homework and do not see the promise of video sites as effective learning tools.

> We have found YouTube to be really frustrating. It's not like our son is watching anything that is inappropriate; it's all just kind of dumb humor. The problem is that kids can get totally lost in it. They take a five-minute study break to "just watch one video," and then it is impossible to resist watching five more videos that show up on the side of the screen. The thing that took some adjustment with the 1-to-1 is that all of a sudden everything was happening in the same place, and it was way too stimulating. We have a rule that "entertainment media" can only be looked at after homework is done and on the weekends. We had to watch over his shoulder a lot when he first got the 1-to-1 to make sure the rule was being followed.
>
> Kimberly, parent of a fifth grader

The reality for this generation of students and the future of their work lives is the need to build skills that help them manage distraction. With the convergence of entertainment and education into a single tool (the 1-to-1 device), kids will always be just one click away from distraction. One of the benefits of a 1-to-1 program is that adults, both teachers and parents, can teach focusing on one task at a time as a fundamental skill.

Chapter 2   Get Set!   Decisions about Specific Issues

> We learned the hard way that YouTube is a social network as well as a place for watching videos. Find out if your child has a YouTube account and, if so, make sure that he or she is posting appropriate material.
>
> Jeff, parent of a sixth grader

This is an important reminder about any site you give your child permission to use. Chances are that the site comes with additional features, and some of the features will likely include social interaction. On video sites where kids are enthusiastic about the content they are watching and possibly creating, it is important to stay engaged and discuss with your child not only the actual video content, but also the conversations that are going on around the videos.

> YouTube is the site that takes up the most time and is most distracting. It's hard, too, because kids often need it for their schoolwork.
>
> Allen, parent of a ninth grader

"Are you studying or messing around?" If this question is being asked too frequently in your house, it's a good idea to check in with your child's school to find out more information about when video sites are actually a part of the curriculum.

Also, you can help your child by breaking down homework tasks by the level of concentration required. This acknowledges the reality of a busy study environment and will help your child to think about concentration as a valuable and limited resource.

Educators Speak

Educators are aware of the challenges that viewing video sites on 1-to-1 devices present to families. The following comments illustrate how video sites force the need for partnership between home and school and how teachers are now increasingly considering what happens outside the classroom as part of their domain.

> Video on the Internet lasts forever—that little camera on a device can do great damage or great good. This is a deeply moral issue rather than a technological one. Yes, the ability to take and post videos is now in everyone's hands, but what each of us chooses to do with that ability will depend upon our moral compass.
>
> Thomas, iPad integration coordinator in Watsonville, California

Kids are excited by their ability to create and share videos. It is an area where impulse control can be compromised in the rush to share with the world. Parents can encourage their kids to have a "24-Hour Rule," in that the child will agree to wait before deciding to post any content to a video site. This teaches the lesson that what feels hilarious at the moment might not be that funny in the morning.

> Just occasionally, keep an eye on what the students are doing. Talk with them about how they use the Internet. Share videos that you like with them.
>
> Blair, principal in São Paulo, Brazil

Parent worries about kids and video sites are understandable. Most often, the worry comes from a good place, which is the desire to protect kids and keep them from getting into uncomfortable or embarrassing situations where they will be in over their heads. Keeping kids safe does not have to be all about setting and enforcing rules. It can also be done through modeling good behavior. Sharing videos and connecting around common areas of interest are excellent ways to share positive feelings and teach lessons about thoughtful communication.

> I encourage parents to have conversations about time management with students. Watching videos can be very time consuming. We know students love to watch music videos and find the latest video craze! Our mission is to be proactive and educate students as much as possible on making good choices on the Internet.
>
> Cari, principal in Conrad, Iowa

By putting a laptop or tablet in a child's hands, schools are saying that video sites and the ability to create and share videos have a place in a child's education. Cari's quote does a good job of describing how 1-to-1 schools can embrace their students' enthusiasm for video sites while remaining in their role as educators. This puts schools in a better position to teach valuable lessons about responsible behavior in the digital age.

Chapter 2 Get Set! Decisions about Specific Issues

Checklist 3

Video Sites

☐ Find out if your child is allowed to upload videos to video sites (such as YouTube) on the 1-to-1 device.

☐ Find out how often video sites will be used for school assignments and how you can tell if your kids are studying (or not) when watching videos.

☐ Find out if there are school rules about the content of videos that can be downloaded or uploaded on the 1-to-1 device. (For example: Are media with explicit lyrics or images allowed?)

☐ Decide if there are home rules about the content of videos that can be downloaded or uploaded on the 1-to-1 device.

The School's Policy

_____
_____
_____
_____
_____

Our Family Policy

_____
_____
_____
_____
_____

Resources: Video Sites

YouTube's Community Guidelines
   www.youtube.com/t/community_guidelines
      YouTube explains its community guidelines.

Vimeo's Community Guidelines
   http://vimeo.com/help/guidelines
      Vimeo explains its community guidelines.

Apps Limit Digital Distractions to Help Users Stay on Task
   http://99u.com/articles/6969/10-Online-Tools-for-Better-Attention-Focus
      There are tech solutions designed to help people of all ages to stay on task when working on an Internet-connected computer or device. This article describes 10 software applications that limit users' digital distractions and contribute to efficient organization and concentration.

Social Networks

What is a social network site? A social network site is an online place for individuals to form groups of loose or strong connections and share information. On social network sites like Facebook, an individual sets up a profile page and shares information in the form of posts. Posts can be still images, text, videos, or links. Interaction takes place through commenting on posts. Both posts and comments can be directed to select individuals or the entire group. Most major social network sites have security settings that allow users to determine how publicly or privately posts and comments are shared. Social network sites often have additional features, such as games, chat (both video and text), and the ability to obtain information about areas of interest.

Parents Speak

Social network sites have not been around that long. For example, Facebook was launched in 2004. In their short history, however, they have made a major impact on childhood and family life. The value of social connections (or who is considered

Chapter 2 Get Set! Decisions about Specific Issues

a friend), the concept of what is appropriate to share publicly versus privately, and the idea of home being a place to be away from peers have all been altered by social network sites. Part of the reason for this huge impact is the way that social network sites fit into the separation and individuation process that is a natural part of childhood development. As younger kids mature into adolescence, they increasingly look to their peer group for feedback and seek out places where there is greater freedom and autonomy. For kids, social network sites have become places to experience the news and events of their lives.

Clearly, this brings up challenges for parents and schools. While parents and schools want kids to have places where they can interact privately with their peer groups, they want to make sure these places are safe, have children's best interests in mind, and have adequate adult supervision. Conscientious parents want to feel a sense of control in making sure their kids are developmentally ready to handle the levels of freedom and autonomy that they've received.

Such safeguards are often hard to achieve on social network sites. The age at which kids use social network sites, such as Facebook (a site intended for kids 13 years and older), keeps getting younger. With kids having greater access to new technologies, parents find it is difficult to keep them from these sites.

As you can see from the parents' quotes that follow, no one has devised a unified message about the "right" way to handle social network sites. Parents need to educate themselves about social network sites and to take a realistic approach to their pervasiveness in kids' lives.

For parents of kids younger than 13, it may be possible to hold off online social networking for a few years and keep kids away from these sites. If your child shows an early interest in social network sites, it is important to find alternative outlets that fit his or her social needs. You may choose an age-appropriate social network site or insist upon greater adult supervision on sites intended for older kids. For parents of adolescents, it is necessary to understand how these sites work, to keep open dialogues going with your teens about how the sites are being used, and to have some safeguards in place that allow for parental supervision.

Get Set! Decisions about Specific Issues — Chapter 2

> I found Facebook to be one of the most confusing parts of getting the 1-to-1. We had kept our daughter off the site when she shared our computer at home, and then when she got the 1-to-1, we let her sign up for an account. It seemed like if she could be responsible for an iPad computer, she could be responsible on Facebook. The problem was it was just too much too soon—having her own iPad and Facebook all at the same time. It was just too much freedom. I wish we had introduced them one at a time.
>
> — Patty, parent of a ninth grader

Patty gives us a good example of too much too soon. In a 1-to-1 environment, it is still possible to start with limits that kids can outgrow. If your child's school allows Facebook and you have held off from giving permission to use the site, there are ways to ease into the world of social networking. You might start by having your child check in with you before adding anyone to a friend list. You can also set up the account with a shared email address and have a shared a password. Once your child has outgrown these limits (or shown the ability to handle more restrictive limits responsibly), you can experiment with allowing greater freedom and autonomy.

> We actually do not let our son use Facebook on the school-issued laptop. He is only allowed to use it for studying purposes, and if he wants to use Facebook, he has to use it on the desktop computer that is in plain sight near the living room.
>
> — Jane, parent of a ninth grader

For families whose kids have access to more than one computer, it is possible to attempt to use the 1-to-1 device for schoolwork only. This often proves difficult over time because of the boundary-blurring nature of the 1-to-1 device, where the line between school and social is never completely clear. It is possible, however, to have an open-door policy (that is, the child's bedroom door stays open) or have a rule that the 1-to-1 device only be used in common family areas.

> Everyone in our family is on Facebook, so it really isn't a big deal. I feel like I know what's going on in my kids' lives and what they are doing online doesn't seem all that different with my kids. The real difference that I see with the 1-to-1 is that it mixes social life and school life. I actually think it makes it easier for my kids to understand when I say, "Do not write anything online that you wouldn't feel comfortable with your teacher, mom, or grandmother seeing."
>
> — Sam, parent of eighth and tenth graders

Parents' who use the same social network sites their kids use have the advantage of a better sense of how these sites work. At the same time, kids use these sites differently, and there are often nuances that parents can miss if they base their sense of what is going on with their child on an adult's experience. For parents who use these sites, good opportunities for conversations about the differences between adults' and kids' experiences on social networks abound.

Educators Speak

1-to-1 schools take different approaches to social network sites. Some schools ban sites like Facebook completely, others allow kids to access the sites but do not use them as part of the curriculum, and some use them as a learning tool.

> We allow Twitter but not Facebook. At this time, Twitter has become an educational tool for us. I would encourage [the parents] to create an account and to closely follow their children. Again, having conversations about appropriate use is critical!
>
> Cari, principal in Conrad, Iowa

If kids' social network site experiences are reserved for only speaking with a narrow peer group, there is little room for influence from others. While the perception has been that it is dangerous for kids to communicate with adults online, there is also a great opportunity for adults to have a positive impact on kids. This is especially true for school projects where adults with a particular expertise can contribute valuable information that often goes far beyond what is available within the four walls of the classroom.

> Check with the age requirements for Facebook. Is your child 13 or older? Monitor usage and review with your child the privacy issues in regard to how much information to make public and what to share.
>
> Douglas, school counselor in Berkeley, California

Security settings on social network sites change frequently, and when settings change, it usually means that more information is made public. While sites like Facebook have become more aware of the need to protect kids' privacy, it is important to stay on top of these changes. Every few months, families should check security settings on social network sites. It is also essential to create secure passwords, change passwords frequently, and remind kids not to share their passwords with friends.

> We encourage parents to let kids use social media, but we also encourage them to talk to their kids about creating a positive digital footprint.
> Blair, principal in São Paulo, Brazil

A digital footprint is the information that accumulates over time about a person online. While some of this information is set up to be private (like bank account information and medical records), the information on social network sites is designed to be viewed by an audience. Remember to check settings and friend lists to have a better handle on who is in the audience. Kids and adults do have control over what the audience sees. Many 1-to-1 schools are taking an active role in teaching kids about how to be sensible curators of their digital footprints. This means cleaning up old information to make sure that it is not embarrassing. It also means building awareness about the limits of privacy online and broadening a child's sense of how information might be viewed over time.

Chapter 2   Get Set!   Decisions about Specific Issues

Checklist 4

Social Networks

☐ Find out if your child is allowed to or expected to use social network sites (such as Facebook and Twitter) on the 1-to-1 device at school.

☐ If the school allows them, find out how often social network sites will be used for school assignments and how you can tell whether your kids are studying (or not) when they're on digital social network sites.

☐ If using social networks is allowed, find out if there are school rules about the kinds of content/comments that can be shared on social network sites.

☐ If social network use is allowed, decide whether you want to establish home rules about the use of social network sites on the 1-to-1 device.

The School's Policy

_____
_____
_____
_____
_____

Our Family Policy

_____
_____
_____
_____
_____

Resources: Social Networks

A Facebook Guide for Parents
www.connectsafely.org/pdfs/fbparents.pdf

    This Facebook guide for parents is useful and free.

Common Sense Media Names Social Networking Sites for Younger Kids
www.commonsensemedia.org/website-lists/social-networking-kids

    Common Sense Media recommends several social network sites for kids who are 14 and younger by age groups (preschoolers 2–4, young kids 5–6, kids 7–8, preteens 9–11, and teens 12–14).

Facebook's Online Safety Basics for Parents
www.facebook.com/safety/groups/parents

    Facebook provides advice and resources for parents about their teens' use of its site.

Facebook's Methods for Reporting and Addressing Abuse
www.facebook.com/help/263149623790594

    Facebook describes the processes for reporting and addressing inappropriate content, harassment, and abuse on its site.

Video Games

Video games are no longer just about shooting things and collecting coins. Video games can now be social, they are diverse enough to appeal to nearly all kids, and they are increasingly being thought of as a learning tool. Video games have become an important part of modern childhood. Kids start playing video games earlier these days, and as kids mature, they grow into and out of games that match their social and emotional development.

Parents Speak

Video games—their content and time spent playing them—present a complicated challenge for parents and kids. While parents often find the games to be a waste of time, kids who enjoy them feel they would rather spend time playing video games than doing anything else for fun. Most parents do not have a problem with kids

Chapter 2 Get Set! Decisions about Specific Issues

spending some time with age-appropriate video games. Yet parents of enthusiastic game players feel frustrated when their kids leave no room for other activities. While the 1-to-1 device provides children with their own place to do schoolwork, it also opens a portal to video games. Navigating this area successfully depends on a child's age and level of interest in playing video games. If your child's time spent playing video games is a source of contention in your home, it is important for you to understand the attraction and set rules and limits that take into account the actual games that your child is playing.

> We have had so many challenges around video games in our family, and the 1-to-1 device just made things more difficult. It felt like it tipped an already precarious balance. We struggled with it for an entire year, and I have to say I was relieved when we turned in the laptop for the summer.
>
> Larry, parent of a seventh grader

Certain kids ("gamers") just love video games. They tend to gravitate toward video games at an early age. If they were left unsupervised, they would spend the whole day (or days) playing. Some of these kids struggle in other areas of their lives, so video games become the place where they excel and feel competent. If this description matches your child, then you've likely experienced the difficult task of setting limits on video game time.

To remove some of the power struggles, parents need to understand the nuances of time for the games their children are playing. For example, social games don't necessarily fit well with the family's schedule. A six o'clock dinner might be the time that friends from another part of the country or world are just logging on to play. You may have an agreement with your daughter that she may spend an hour or two playing video games after she finishes her homework, but when the time limit is up, the game she's been waiting an hour to play has just begun. You do not have to plan your family's life around video game time, but if you can discuss how to set practical guidelines on game time with some credibility and empathy, you'll be able to work with your child and defuse or prevent power struggles.

> We have lots of gamers in our house, including my husband. We're pretty lenient about video games. The main thing for us is that the kids turn off the games without a fight when we ask them to come to dinner or to do something else.
>
> Julie, parent of a seventh grader

Setting limits and having rules in place can be much easier than sticking to them. Parents' and children's negotiations around living with limits and rules are tougher than writing them down. Getting kids to turn off video games after the agreed-upon time limit has elapsed is a common area where conflicts spike into yelling and screaming.

Soft transitions between game time and family time or game time and bedtime are easier to make when they are part of the routine. For younger kids, it can be helpful to schedule video game time between other events. For example, video game time might be between breakfast and leaving for school. That way, everyone has a predictable, clear way of knowing exactly when games can be played and what needs to be done. A morning rule for young children could be something like this: Once the breakfast dishes are cleared and school clothes and shoes are on, it is time to play video games. Then, when it is time to leave for school, video games are turned off. For older kids and teens, if you find yourselves getting embroiled in conflicts, it might help to use special timers or software that shuts the computer off at certain times.

> We have a rule where our kids have to ask us before they download any apps, even the free ones. With the Apple 1-to-1, they got their own account on iTunes, and it was possible for them to download whatever they wanted. This was a change because they used to have to ask for a parent to put in the password when they wanted to buy games, and now they have that power. We put a rule in place [that each child may spend only a certain amount on music and games], and it is working out pretty well. We also spot-check their apps to make sure they haven't downloaded anything we don't want them to download.
>
> Kimberly, parent of a fifth grader

No agreement with your children about choosing appropriate video games and setting time limits is going to allow you to set it and forget it. Parents must stay engaged, and kids need ongoing, predictable ways to check in with parents. It may be difficult for parents to stay vigilant, and kids may object; however, kids need to be held responsible for their choices and behavior. While kids may complain about their family's rules, they appreciate their parents' setting boundaries and paying attention to them. When parents acknowledge their children's positive behavior and adherence to the family's guidelines, kids will generally try to be even more responsible to prove their maturity and readiness for increased independence. The 1-to-1 Child and Parent Agreement (Appendix A, Form A.3) will get you started and provides a clear explanation to your child about how you plan to stay engaged with guidelines and limits.

Chapter 2 Get Set! Decisions about Specific Issues

Educators Speak

Video games have a place in a 1-to-1 learning environment for reasons that are central to the goals of 1-to-1 learning. On a practical level, any time children are given their own laptops or tablets, regardless of how many restrictions are put in place, they will find a way to play video games. It is easier for educators to acknowledge the reality that kids will play video games than to spend their time trying to stop them from playing. Also, the goals of 1-to-1 learning share many qualities that are found in today's video games. The exploration, collaboration, and enthusiasm that kids bring to video games are seen as crucial elements in educating students to take advantage of the opportunities of the 21st century. As the following educators point out, achieving these goals is about harnessing video games as learning tools and helping kids to know when and why to put video games away.

> Restricting gaming is one choice. But that may not be a fight worth fighting. New research in education is showing that gaming can accelerate learning. Therefore, perhaps the better approach is to define appropriate and inappropriate times and places for gaming and then to enforce those definitions. Solitaire on a computer is as much a game as solitaire with a deck of cards. When is it appropriate to take out a deck of cards and start playing solitaire? When is it inappropriate? We have to translate the technology into situations where we already understand what the rules of behavior ought to be and then apply them to the current technology.
>
> Thomas, iPad integration coordinator in Watsonville, California

Parents rarely think of playing video games as an important activity. Video games often don't have a real place in family life. Games online are treated as something to be done in a spare moment or after all other important activities have been completed. This attitude can get in the way of kids' understanding the appropriate time and place for video games. Not only can it turn video games into the forbidden digital fruit, it can also deprive kids of the opportunity to see their parents manage video games in the same way they manage the other activities of family life. Just as 1-to-1 schools are making room for video games because of the lessons they can teach, parents can teach lessons at home about video games by including them as part of the ongoing conversation about family life.

An area of concern for parents is the amount of violence and inappropriate images kids are exposed to in video games. Kids will often say that they understand the difference between what happens on the screen and what happens in real life and that games are helpful for releasing feelings of frustration in a safe place. This is a valid point because kids make sense of complicated issues as they play throughout their development. This does not mean parents have to condone video games they find objectionable. Some families will decide to keep particular kinds of games out of their homes, and others will set limits based on ratings systems, such as the ESRB ratings. While allowing or disallowing certain games is a decision for parents to make, it is important that they talk about the personal values they hold for themselves and their families. Parents need to explain what makes certain games objectionable when they forbid their children to play them. They also need to discuss with their kids (in age-appropriate ways) alternative points of view that illustrate their areas of concern.

> **ESRB Ratings**
>
> The ratings established by the Entertainment Software Rating Board (ESRB) encompass three main areas to assist adults in evaluating video games and apps: (1) "rating categories" for age appropriateness comprise seven categories, including EC for early childhood, E for everyone, E10+ for ages 10 and up, T for teens ages 13 and up, M for mature people ages 17 and up, AO for adults only, and RP for rating pending; (2) "content descriptors" focus on various levels of violence, profanity, sexual content, crude humor, and other ethically questionable or suggestive behaviors; and (3) "interactive elements" describe the levels of personal information, location, and interaction shared by gamers and apps users.

> We decide which games are allowed by using the ESRB ratings system. We do not allow games rated T or higher on our 1-to-1 laptops.
>
> Bonnie, director of technology in San Rafael, California

Chapter 2   Get Set!   Decisions about Specific Issues

> We recommend that restrictions are put on apps so that only age-appropriate apps can be accessed. Some parents choose to restrict the ability to download any app that is not school approved. We support parents. Whatever the rule at home is, we support it at school.
>
> —Kelly, technology integration consultant in Lone Tree, Colorado

Video games are now social. This means that kids can play together from separate locations and can collaborate or compete within games. This is one reason why a game can quickly become popular within a 1-to-1 school community. When this happens, the video game of the moment will become the "must have" game in your household. This requires parents and schools to stay in closer contact. Parents need to keep lines of communication open with their child's school. Schools want to know what is going on at home and use the information as a way to keep an eye on how the 1-to-1 device is being used within the student community. Parents are not alone in struggling with whether to allow their kids to play a specific social video game. When schools hear about parents' concerns, they can help address the situation. As a wide variety of video games are available, school technology directors or consultants can usually suggest alternative games that have appropriate content and fit within the school's learning objectives.

Checklist 5

Video Games

☐ Find out if your child is allowed to play video games on the 1-to-1 device at school and is expected to play them at home.

☐ If video games are allowed, find out how often the games will be used for school assignments and how you can tell whether or not your kids are fulfilling class assignments when playing video games.

☐ If games are allowed, find out whether there are school rules about the kinds of video games that can be played. (For example, in addition to learning games, are violent games allowed?)

☐ If certain types of learning and social games are allowed, decide whether you need to establish home rules about playing these video games on the 1-to-1 device.

The School's Policy

_____
_____
_____
_____
_____

Our Family Policy

_____
_____
_____
_____
_____

Chapter 2   Get Set!   Decisions about Specific Issues

Resources: Video Games

Apple's Parental Controls for Kids' Time on Computer or Apps
www.apple.com/findouthow/mac/#parentalcontrols

> The Apple operating system allows parents to set up controls for the amount of time kids can spend using the computer or using specific applications (including the Internet and games).

Windows' Parental Controls for Kids' Time on Computer or Apps
http://windows.microsoft.com/en-US/windows7/products/features/parental-controls

> The Windows operating system allows parents to set up controls for the amount of time kids can spend using the computer or using specific applications (including the Internet and games).

How to Make Parental Controls More Effective
http://netsecurity.about.com/od/security101/a/8-Ways-To-Kid-Proof-Your-Internet-Parental-Controls.htm

> See eight tips, such as securing your home router and using parental controls on games and mobile devices, for protecting your child online.

ESRB Video Games' Ratings Explained on Wikipedia
http://en.wikipedia.org/wiki/Entertainment_Software_Rating_Board

> This Wikipedia page provides information about the Entertainment Software Rating Board (ESRB). Similar to the ratings system used by the movie industry, the ESRB reviews video games and provides guidelines for age appropriateness. It rates games for violence, sexual situations, profanity, and other types of content and has ratings for levels of interaction expected of players.

ESRB Video Games' Ratings
www.esrb.org/ratings

> For further information on the Entertainment Software Rating Board, consult the ESRB website.

Common Sense Media's Advice for Parents on Educational and Entertainment Apps
www.commonsensemedia.org/advice-for-parents/
apps-101-what-know-you-download

> Common Sense Media provides practical advice about downloading applications (apps). Many apps are free, including entertaining and competitive games; educational games; and social networks, like Facebook, which itself contains other apps. Some apps may appear to be free but are designed to sell merchandise or to sell upgrades to the original app that was free.

Common Sense Media Advises Setting Screen-Time Limits
www.commonsensemedia.org/advice-for-parents/
dont-touch-dial-tips-limiting-screen-time

> Common Sense Media offers parents tips for setting screen-time limits, that is, how much time kids may be allowed to use computers, TVs, games, and movies. For another helpful article, see the link to "Setting Computer Limits Tips" (www.commonsensemedia.org/advice-for-parents/setting-computer-limits-tips).

Video, Voice, and Text Chatting

What is online chatting? Chatting software allows synchronous communication through Internet-connected devices. Chatting can be done in the form of text, voice, and video. It is also possible to use chat to communicate with large or small groups of people in different physical locations. Popular chat programs include gChat and iChat.

Parents Speak

Many parents realize what a game changer the 1-to-1 device is when they first see their child video chatting with a classmate who is using an identical laptop or tablet from across the city or town. They see how the 1-to-1 device is both a learning tool and a social toy and realize that it will become a central part of their child's life.

Chapter 2   Get Set!   Decisions about Specific Issues

> The video chatting seemed like too much in the beginning. I think they were all just really excited to have this new toy. It is pretty cool; I would have been excited if I could have talked to my friends like that when I was a kid. After the thrill of it wore off, the kids settled into it, and I've seen them use it really responsibly.
>
> Sue, parent of an eighth grader

When the 1-to-1 device first arrives, keep in mind that the novelty of chatting will likely wear off. Waves of enthusiasm for technology are going to come and go and come back again throughout your child's development. Take a long-term approach when a new technology wave like chatting sweeps through your home.

It is also important to have basic ground rules about safety, trust, and respect in place to help you navigate. Take the time to learn about chatting while your child is excited about it. Exercise your due diligence by talking to the school and other parents about chatting and set sensible parameters that are based on other social technologies where you already have experience. Here are some examples of sensible parameters about chatting:

- Know who your child is chatting with.
- Ask that your child check in with you before chatting with anyone new.
- Make it clear where and when chatting can happen.
- Talk about the potential for meanness and harassment within group and individual chats.

"Keep it in a public place" is an often-repeated rule about kids and technologies like the 1-to-1 device.

> We now have a central place in our kitchen where the iPad has to be stored and charged at night. Our daughter was forgetting to bring it charged up to school. If we have her leave it in the kitchen, we know that she won't be chatting with her friends all night.
>
> Julie, parent of a seventh grader

Keeping the device in a public place is an important rule and one that families should try to follow. With that said, the rule is only as strong as the extent to which it is followed. This is really about secretiveness and how your children behave when you are curious or concerned about what is going on in their lives.

Get Set! Decisions about Specific Issues Chapter 2

If your child closes the 1-to-1 device frequently when you approach or quickly changes the window on the screen, it is important to address secretiveness directly and figure out why activities on the screen need to be a secret from parents. It is also necessary for parents to establish sensible boundaries around the 1-to-1 device and to provide their child with a sense that he or she has an age- and developmentally appropriate amount of privacy.

> We've actually found the video chat to be great. We live far away from the school, and it's a great way for our son to stay in contact with his classmates. Some of his teachers even have "office hours" when they are online for questions, and that has been great, too.
>
> Allen, parent of a ninth grader

Keep in mind the educational possibilities of being able to communicate with peers, friends, and teachers outside school. When used appropriately, chatting software can make homework far more engaging and interactive. It can be looked at more like an age-appropriate version of studying in a college dormitory group, where students have access to peers in a setting that creates greater formal and informal learning opportunities.

Educators Speak

When schools adopt 1-to-1 programs, they are making a statement about the value of new technologies in education. They are saying that schools have a role in teaching a new set of skills, and these skills are about more than just the traditional realms of learning. They are also about teaching safety, trust, and respect for the digital age. In the quotes that follow, educators highlight how they are getting involved in teaching these values to their students using text, voice, and video chatting.

> We monitor all conversation on iChat. I would encourage parents to have conversations with their children about iChat and to find out who they are conversing with. I would encourage them to have discussions about why it is easier to be mean online. Also, have they ever felt uncomfortable when chatting with someone? It is important for students to understand that personal information stays personal!
>
> Cari, principal in Conrad, Iowa

Chapter 2 Get Set! Decisions about Specific Issues

There is a great deal to learn about privacy in the digital age and how this knowledge can be used to avoid getting caught up in drama, meanness, and harassment. Communicating in a digital environment is different from communicating in person, and these differences can have a big impact on a child's life. With chatting, as in any form of digital communication, kids can never be fully assured that what they are sharing is private. What a child says can be recorded and taken out of context or altered. And once something is captured digitally, it has the potential to spread quickly across the Internet. Furthermore, the safety of communicating behind a screen and not face-to-face can lower inhibitions and make kids more likely to say things that they would not say in other settings. Understanding these differences is now an important part of growing up. In the digital age, kids need as many adults as possible to help them to make sense of privacy.

> Monitor usage, especially during homework time.
> — Douglas, school counselor in Berkeley, California

Working in the more social environment that the 1-to-1 device creates has limitations. While the 1-to-1 device can be great for gathering information and getting input from peers and teachers, kids need some quiet time to do more focused work. Shutting off the Internet connection on the 1-to-1 device or setting aside clear amounts of time to be spent "disconnected" can help your child to find quiet, individual study time.

> We use iPads—removing the built-in chatting feature isn't worth the hassle. Most of these issues revolve around behavior rather than technology, and then encouraging and enforcing proper behavior. There are actually some very positive educational applications for chatting.
> — Thomas, iPad integration coordinator in Watsonville, California

"Built-in" is not only about the equipment itself, but also what kids come to see as the normal tools at their disposal. In a 1-to-1 learning environment, kids become accustomed to the ability to share resources with peers and teachers through the use of chat. This "built-in" knowledge will likely serve them well in the world of work, where it is becoming common for projects to be completed by people in various locations.

Checklist 6

Chatting

☐ Find out if your child is allowed to or expected to use video, voice, or text chat (such as gChat and iChat) on the 1-to-1 device.

☐ If it is allowed, find out how often chatting will be used for school assignments and how you can tell if your kids are studying when chatting.

☐ If chatting is allowed, find out if there are school rules about the kinds of content/comments that may be shared while chatting on the 1-to-1 device.

☐ If it is allowed, decide whether home rules need to be made about what can be shared while chatting on the 1-to-1 device.

The School's Policy

_____
_____
_____
_____
_____

Our Family Policy

_____
_____
_____
_____
_____

Chapter 2   Get Set!   Decisions about Specific Issues

Resources: Video, Voice, and Text Chatting

Google's Chat Features
> http://support.google.com/chat/bin/answer.py?hl=en&answer=161934
>> Google's chat features are explained on this site.

Apple's Video Chat Software
> www.apple.com/ios/facetime
>> Apple's video chat software, Facetime, is explained here.

Skype's Video Chat Features
> http://about.skype.com/product.html
>> Skype's video chat features are explained on its site.

Facebook's Chat Features
> www.facebook.com/help/332952696782239
>> Facebook's basic chat features are explained on this page.

Facebook's Video Calling Chat Feature
> www.facebook.com/videocalling
>> Facebook's video chat feature, video calling, is explained here.

Ergonomics and Sleep

What is ergonomics? Ergonomics is the science of workplace efficiency. Ergonomics takes into account how all the variables of our physical environment and the tools we use, like the 1-to-1 device, impact our bodies and minds. In an ergonomically efficient or correct environment, support is given so that the tools used are doing as little physical damage to the body and mind as possible. Providing a more upright chair, a keyboard for a tablet, or a different mouse for a computer are examples of how ergonomics can be used to alleviate repetitive stress injuries and help our bodies and minds to function more efficiently. Sleep should also be considered as an ergonomics issue. Studies clearly show that students' behavior, ability to think clearly, and academic performance are affected by poor sleep or a lack of sleep.

Parents Speak

Ergonomics is often an afterthought. Most people do not consider making physical adjustments to their work environments until they begin to notice strain or pain.

> Honestly, we don't pay much attention to it [ergonomics], but I really think we should. It's a lot of hours in front of a screen and a lot of sitting.
>
> Sue, parent of an eighth grader

Spending time outdoors is important. Back when parents and grandparents were growing up, getting together with friends often meant gathering outdoors. In a 1-to-1 environment where kids have more social opportunities indoors, families can adjust by spending more time outside the house and in nature.

> Our whole family spends a great deal of time on computers. We try to model getting up and getting outdoors.
>
> Kimberly, parent of a fifth grader

Parents whose children use a 1-to-1 device at home need to assess how using the device affects their child's posture. Parents can make ergonomic adjustments so that desks and chairs, lighting, and keyboards are situated at the best angles to prevent repetitive stress injuries and back and neck pain.

> We give our daughter constant reminders about sitting up straight. We also bought a mouse and keyboard for the iPad because it seemed like it was better for her wrist.
>
> Patty, parent of a ninth grader

It is also important to remind kids to stay hydrated while they are working and to put the 1-to-1 device away while eating meals.

Work with your children to set up predictable times when they can get up and stretch, for example, while waiting for a video to load or as part of switching tasks. When parents and kids are working at home on computers and 1-to-1 devices, they can remind each other to get up from their chairs every hour.

Chapter 2   Get Set!   Decisions about Specific Issues

The 1-to-1 device can also interfere with your child's getting enough sleep due to using the device late at night or early in the morning.

> We didn't have trouble with bedtime. We had trouble with the time our son was waking up in the morning after he got the 1-to-1. He was always tired and we found out that he was waking up at five in the morning to play his favorite video game. I wake up at six-thirty in the morning and it took me a while to realize that this was going on. Instead of setting a bedtime, we had to set up a wakeup time.
>
> Steven, parent of a ninth grader

Help your child to establish good bedtime routines. This should include not using the 1-to-1 device in bed, storing the device outside the bedroom during sleep time, and establishing a wind-down period of 30 minutes to an hour when the device is not used before going to sleep.

> One of the big topics around our house when we got the 1-to-1 was about how it was impacting the amount of sleep our daughter was getting a night. With a study environment that is full of distractions, we were finding that she was taking a much longer time to complete her homework. This meant that "homework time" was eating into her sleep time. We have had to set up firmer rules about study time and bedtime and drop an extracurricular activity to make it possible for our daughter to get eight hours of sleep a night.
>
> Josephina, parent of a seventh grader

Educators Speak

Schools are also realizing the physical side of 1-to-1 programs. They are seeing how the choices they make about which equipment to use has effects beyond just the social, emotional, and academic realms of a child's life. It is crucial for educators and parents to consider how the physical use of the 1-to-1 equipment affects kids.

> Don't think that you can apply any of your adult understanding to new touch devices. For example, today's adults were all taught to type by touch. The keys were arranged to favor speed with respect to frequency of a letter's use. Today's virtual keyboards do not function on touch but on sight and memory. Some of today's virtual keyboards work better with thumbs than fingers. We ought to let today's youth reinvent the keyboard's layout to reflect a style of typing that is more efficiently paired with how they are using the keyboard.
>
> Thomas, iPad integration coordinator in Watsonville, California

If your child is using a 1-to-1 tablet, remember that the tablet is a different tool than a laptop or computer. Set up a work environment at home that takes into account the tablet's screen-based keyboard, or consider purchasing a mouse and keyboard for the tablet.

> As educators we spend a great deal of time thinking about how to best utilize the laptops for learning, but we don't focus enough on how the laptops are physically being used. You see students around school, and they are clearly sitting in ways that are bad for their bodies. At our school we address this, and we also educate our students on how to best use the equipment for their bodies' well-being. Our goal is to help students develop good habits and for this generation, who are going to spend the majority of their work lives in front of some kind of computer screen, they need to get in the habit of thinking about ergonomics. All schools should be putting resources into teaching proper ergonomics, and for 1-to-1 schools this is especially true. At home, parents should make it a priority to teach their kids proper physical use of the 1-to-1.
>
> John, head of school in Walnut Creek, California

Get a sense from your child's school about the amount of class time kids are spending on the 1-to-1 device and how many repetitive tasks are taking place. Also, find out how the school addresses ergonomics. You can make sure your child receives consistent messages from both home and school on the importance of using the 1-to-1 device in ways that are not harmful physically.

Box 2.1 Tips from an ergonomic consultant

Good Posture in the Digital Age

Parents need to be concerned about their child's physical comfort when working at a computer. Children's bodies are resilient in the short term; however, wear and tear can show up later in life.

The child's torso, neck, and head should be on a vertical plane: watch out for a child's head being tilted forward in order to read the screen. Remediations might include

- Providing reading glasses specifically for computer use
- Moving the monitor up or down or replacing it with a larger one
- Encouraging better posture

If the child is a touch typist, the midline of the top of the child's forearm should be aligned with the middle knuckle of the hand and with the top of the hand, resulting in a relaxed position. Remediations might include

- Raising of a height-adjustable chair
- Lowering of the desk
- Providing a wrist rest

Frequent use of a mouse in a manner that causes bending the wrist in the direction of the little finger (ulnar deviation) needs to be avoided. Remediations might include

- Ensuring 2-minute breaks every 15 minutes
- Replacing a mouse with a track-ball
- Raising of a height-adjustable chair or lowering of the desk
- Providing a wrist rest
- Teaching wrist-neutral ways to use a mouse

If a child is experiencing soreness or pain in the wrist, back, or neck or is experiencing eye strain—and if the remediations you try do not stop the symptoms—an appropriate medical professional should be consulted immediately.

Jack Litewka
Ergonomic consultant, Berkeley, California

Get Set! Decisions about Specific Issues   Chapter 2

We may have quickly transitioned into a 24/7 digital world, but our bodies are still the same. Getting enough sleep and having good physical habits when using the tools of work are age-old lessons that kids of every generation need to learn.

> Parents have to know when their child is actually going to sleep. When a student is struggling in school and I talk to the parents, I always ask about sleep routines. I often find that parents are going to sleep before their child and have no idea about the actual time the child is getting to bed, or they are not paying enough attention to sleep routines. It is important for families to talk about proper sleep routines and set limits around bed times. During adolescence, sleep is so important for social and emotional well-being and for school performance.
>
> Janet, principal in Berkeley, California

Chapter 2 Get Set! Decisions about Specific Issues

Checklist 7

Ergonomics and Sleep

☐ Find out about any resources that your school might provide to ensure proper ergonomics. For example, will the school provide a mouse or trackball for the 1-to-1 device?

☐ Decide if you need to purchase any additional equipment necessary to ensure proper ergonomics, such as an adjustable chair, desk, mouse, trackball, or wrist pad.

☐ Set up your child's workspace and discuss proper ergonomics.

☐ Talk to your kids about sleep habits and set smart limits to make sure they are not using the 1-to-1 device at times when they should be sleeping.

☐ Establish home rules regarding where and how the 1-to-1 device is going to be used to ensure proper ergonomics. For example, is it OK to use the device in bed? How long should your child sit without standing up to take a break?

The School's Policy

_____

_____

_____

_____

Our Family Policy

_____

_____

_____

_____

Resources: Ergonomics and Sleep

Ergonomically Healthy Posture at the Computer
www.youtube.com/watch?v=TGx8yfiNvzk

> Using clever graphic designs, a short video, "Computer Posture," demonstrates proper ergonomics for kids and adults as they use tablets, desktop and laptop computers.

Apple's Ergonomics Tips
www.apple.com/about/ergonomics

> Apple provides tips for proper ergonomics.

Stretching App
www.stretchclock.com/more

> StretchClock is an app for both the Windows and Apple operating systems that tracks how long you have been sitting in front of the computer screen and provides video stretching exercises.

Standing Desks
www.nytimes.com/2012/12/02/business/stand-up-desks-gaining-favor-in-the-workplace.html?_r=0

> This *New York Times* article provides some good research and resources for standing desks and also tread desks (yes, desks with treadmills). While this may seem a bit extreme, the article does a good job of describing the benefits of avoiding long periods hunched over a computer.

Microsoft's Ergonomics Tips
www.microsoft.com/hardware/en-us/support/healthy-computing-guide

> Microsoft provides tips for proper ergonomics.

Teens Need More Sleep!
www.pbs.org/wgbh/pages/frontline/shows/teenbrain/from/sleep.html

> Sarah Spinks' article provides an interesting overview of how the body's circadian rhythms affect sleep patterns, especially those of teens. Teens need 9 hours and 15 minutes of sleep per night, yet most do not get nearly that much.

Sleep Deficits May Impair Kids' Cognitive Functioning
http://nymag.com/news/features/38951

> Po Bronson's article warns that a lack of sleep can impair kids' cognitive functioning.

Chapter 3

Go!

Guidelines for the Five Biggest Challenges

There are five key areas where parents and kids experience the most difficulty when it comes to 1-to-1 devices at home. This chapter helps clarify these issues and provides guidelines to resolve problems.

Chapter 3   Go!   Guidelines for the Five Biggest Challenges

The top five areas that cause difficulty are

1. Who takes responsibility for the 1-to-1 device?
2. What do families need to understand about the 1-to-1 study environment?
3. How do families set limits on a boundary-blurring device?
4. What's the right amount of privacy?
5. How much screen time is the right amount?

These questions were already difficult when families were dealing with family-owned computers, devices, and game players. The 1-to-1 device complicates matters by introducing into the mix the school and schoolwork.

Guidelines that are clearly explained will make it easier for parents to have realistic attitudes toward the device and to find the right balance on the continuum between being too permissive and overly strict.

Who Takes Responsibility for the 1-to-1 Device?

The 1-to-1 device is school property; it is handed over to your child at the beginning of the school year, and ultimately it is your child's and your responsibility. This makes the answer to the question, "Who takes responsibility for the 1-to-1 device?" a complicated one.

Answering this question successfully requires taking into account school, child, and home in decisions about the 1-to-1 device. Your home rules and personal values need to have a place in how the device is used. Your child's social, emotional, and educational development need to be taken into account. And, finally, each school's learning objectives and philosophy about its 1-to-1 program have to be understood and followed.

Making this all work together takes parental engagement, clear guidelines, and good communication between home and school. Figure 3.1 illustrates how this looks in the real world. You can use it to remember these key aspects when decisions about your child and the 1-to-1 device need to be made.

Figure 3.1 Who takes responsibility for the 1-to-1 device?

Continued

| Chapter 3 | Go! Guidelines for the Five Biggest Challenges

Figure 3.1 Who takes responsibility for the 1-to-1 device? *Continued*

68   1-to-1 at Home   A Parent's Guide to School-Issued Laptops and Tablets

Go! Guidelines for the Five Biggest Challenges   Chapter 3

What Do Families Need to Understand about the 1-to-1 Study Environment?

The 1-to-1 study environment requires parents to get comfortable having one foot in the future and another in their past. 1-to-1 learning promises to educate a new generation of learners who are prepared for our digital future. At the same time, kids need to learn important lessons from our analog past that offered greater opportunities to think deeply because there were fewer distractions. Creating a study environment that makes room for both kinds of learning is the goal. To do this successfully, schools and parents need to be more explicit about time and make room for conversations about trust to better understand the thinking and communication skills necessary to get the most out of the 1-to-1 study environment.

Figure 3.2 Understanding the 1-to-1 environment

Continued

Figure 3.2 Understanding the 1-to-1 environment *Continued*

How Do Families Set Limits on a Boundary-Blurring Device?

One of the more confusing aspects of the 1-to-1 device being school property but being in your home is how it can disrupt areas of already established rules and limits. Taking away kids' access to technology (such as video games, Internet, cell phones, etc.) as a form of punishment is one way that parents often enforce the breaking of rules or limits. With the 1-to-1 device, however, taking away technology as a form of punishment becomes complicated. Students' schoolwork needs to get done on the device, and educators have said that there is value in your child having access to technology for social as well as educational purposes.

For parents, one of the most complicated and often frustrating aspects of having the 1-to-1 device at home is not being able to rely on old ways of setting rules and limits. Figure 3.3 illustrates the difficulties of taking away the 1-to-1 device and alternative options for setting rules and limits.

Figure 3.3 Rules and limits may need to be revised.

Strategies to Use Instead of Taking Away the 1-to-1 Device

- Limit 1-to-1 device use to public family areas where you can supervise.
- Turn in the 1-to-1 device to parents before bedtime or during specific weekend hours.
- Communicate with your child's school to clarify mandatory schoolwork.
- Limit use to mandatory schoolwork at home.
- Restrict playing time for a specific game or access to a specific social network site where your child is having the most difficulty following limits and rules.

What's the Right Amount of Privacy?

Digital technologies have transformed the notion of privacy. In a short period of time, a tremendous amount of personal information has been converted into digital form. Information in a digital form is easier to use, understand, manipulate, disseminate, and store. This is great when it comes to being able to access banking information, but it is worrisome and possibly dangerous when it comes to kids sharing information about themselves. The 1-to-1 device provides kids with a more personal space, and in this space they will be creating digital information as they work and play. Knowing how much privacy to grant kids in a digital world is not an easy judgment. Figure 3.4 lays out some guidelines about how parents can determine the right amount of privacy in their home.

Figure 3.4 Guidelines for determining privacy limits

Continued

Figure 3.4 Guidelines for determining privacy limits *Continued*

How Much Screen Time Is the Right Amount?

The first question parents often want answered about kids and new technologies has to do with time: "How much time is the right amount when it comes to playing video games, accessing the Internet, and using cell phones?" Figure 3.5 (page 76) introduces the "CALCULTR" to help answer this question.

Most commonly, parents feel their child spends too much time with technology, so they want to set time limits. Figure 3.5 illustrates that comparing screen time to nonscreen time with the help of the CALCULTR gives parents the information they need to more successfully navigate in a 1-to-1 environment.

With a 1-to-1 program, schools place value on digital learning. This adds an additional factor into finding answers to the time question. In truth, there is not a single right answer or right amount of time. Figuring out time is more of an art than a science. To find answers that fit, parents need to look at kids and screens in a different light while keeping the CALCULTR factors in mind:

- Content
- Age
- Level of maturity
- Creativity
- Understand context
- Listen and learn
- Turn off
- Role model

Chapter 3   Go!   Guidelines for the Five Biggest Challenges

Figure 3.5 CALCULTR for determining screen time

There is no specific "right amount" of time. It's better to focus on what is in balance with your family's culture, values, and sense of a healthy lifestyle. Counting hours and minutes on a clock is not a flexible enough tool for measuring the variety of ways kids might be spending their screen time.

Instead, try using the CALCULTR. You might add, subtract, multiply, and divide in order to find the right amount for your own family.

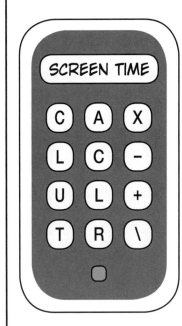

CONTENT— The actual media and messages that are on the screen are as important as the amount of time kids spend online.

LEVEL OF MATURITY— Help choose content that fits with your child's ability to process the media and messages that appear on the screen.

UNDERSTAND CONTEXT— What your children watch, who they play with, and where they watch and play are important.

TURN OFF— Find ways to turn off technology as a family. Now that technology is always with us and some children would rather play games than disconnect, families can decide to have designated times away from screens for individual quiet time or family social times.

AGE— Make sure that the content of the activity is age appropriate for your child.

CREATIVITY— Encourage creative uses of technology. Help your child to make a distinction between consuming and creating media.

LISTEN AND LEARN— Take time to understand your child's likes and dislikes. Especially understand the area where your child has trouble separating from the game or site.

ROLE MODEL— Watch your own media use and the messages that you give to your child about the importance of always being connected.

Chapter 4

Stop!
Reset If Something Goes Wrong

The first three chapters of this guidebook are designed to help you get off on the right foot with the 1-to-1 program at home. This chapter will help you to be prepared in the event that something goes wrong.

Chapter 4   Stop!   Reset If Something Goes Wrong

The 1-to-1 device is by nature a boundary-blurring tool. The 1-to-1 device blurs the boundaries between

- Home and school
- Tool and toy
- Work and play

As the 1-to-1 device makes all of these boundaries less distinct than they were before the devices existed, it is important for parents to be in a good position to be able to judge what is normal and what might be a cause for concern. Parents also may need to prepare for some of the ways their house rules may be disrupted by the 1-to-1 device. Once parents have a sense of the appropriate concerns and rules that fit with the 1-to-1 learning environment, this chapter provides a protocol for "hitting the reset button" if something goes wrong.

Keep in mind that the majority of these issues will not come up for most families, but it is important to understand things that can go wrong and to explore ways of addressing problems should they come up.

There are three levels of issues that may come up in a 1-to-1 situation:

- Typical issues
- Issues requiring adult attention
- Red flags

Let's explore these issues in ascending order of seriousness.

Typical Issues

The following list describes typical behaviors kids may display toward 1-to-1 devices and learning in general.

Your child

- Is fascinated by age-appropriate video games.
- Is engaged with age-appropriate online worlds and social network sites.
- Has difficulty staying focused or on task.
- Is concerned about his/her online reputation.
- Wants to spend free time on the 1-to-1 device.

- Shows no interest in technology and little or no interest in using the 1-to-1 device for nonschool-related activities.

While these are typical behaviors and areas of interest for kids who are growing up with new technologies, any one of them requires your observation and participation. Too often kids receive the message from adults that what happens online is unimportant or a nuisance. Each one of the typical behaviors listed above offers opportunities to better understand your children and their thoughts and feelings. This is especially true for kids who feel passionate about video games, online worlds, and social network sites. You may wish that your children were passionate about activities such as playing the piano or pursuing academic interests, but passion is still passion. Thus parents need to be careful not to send the message that being passionate or enthusiastic about online activities is bad.

When children have difficulties focusing on schoolwork and staying on task, parents need to realize that these normal behaviors are especially complicated in a 1-to-1 environment. Empathize with the challenges that the 1-to-1 device creates and make your years of experience available to your children as they develop their ability to focus and to stay on task.

Above all, leave lines of communication open, and remember that these behaviors are normal not only for kids but also for many adults.

Issues Requiring Adult Attention

The following behaviors necessitate a conversation with your child and may require direct contact with the school to establish a clearer understanding of the issues.

Your child

- Wants to take apart or change the operating system or software on the device.
- Tries to get around school or home Internet safety/monitoring software.
- Engages in inappropriate social interactions (e.g., disparaging remarks) with others online through the 1-to-1 device.
- Accesses inappropriate websites or online content.
- Is secretive and refuses to give parents access to what is happening on the 1-to-1 device.
- Signs up for sites, games, or software without asking parents' permission.

Chapter 4 Stop! Reset If Something Goes Wrong

These items cover areas where children are testing their boundaries. Kids normally explore boundaries and push up against rules and limits. However, parents need to respond in ways that let children know their parents are paying attention, their parents will find fair ways to respond to boundaries being tested, and their parents will provide clear explanations why limits or rules are in place. (Good reasons to approach the school are to get support on how you can be in a better position to pay attention, respond, and get clear on why limits are in place.)

When children are interested in how technology works, they may attempt to change the operating system or software on the 1-to-1 device. This is off limits because it creates headaches for the school's technology department and can prevent the 1-to-1 device from functioning properly. If your child shows an interest in this area, try to work with the school to find alternative outlets for exploring how to fix and maintain computers and other technological devices.

When it comes to accessing inappropriate sites and content, kids need timely, consistent parent input. If your child tests the boundaries in this area, you should take the time to understand the thoughts and feelings behind your child's decisions. Try to have these conversations at times and places that allow for open dialogue when you and your child are not likely to overreact.

Secretiveness and deceptive behaviors can be handled as trust issues. With the 1-to-1 device, trust is among the school, parents, and kids. All three parties' points of view should be considered. If parents decide to place additional limits on kids' 1-to-1 device use to stop these behaviors, the limits should be realistic for home and school.

Inappropriate social interactions often need to be considered as a systemic problem and addressed with the school's help or with input from other parents. The 1-to-1 program requires a new level of collaboration between homes and school. When this works, it can have dramatic, positive effects on the social climate of a school community. When both school and home are involved, negative social interactions that push limits can be quickly addressed and dealt with before they turn into larger issues of harassment and bullying.

Red Flags

The following require immediate action from parents.

Your child

- Is involved in harassing or bullying others on the 1-to-1 device.
- Uses the 1-to-1 device to cheat or plagiarize others' work.
- Intentionally damages or breaks the 1-to-1 device.
- Has inappropriate relationships online.
- Is compulsively involved in a digital activity (games, browsing, music) to the exclusion of schoolwork and normal social interactions.
- Goes out of bounds or commits illegal activities (e.g., pirating copyrighted material, gambling) on the 1-to-1 device.
- Makes inappropriate purchases without parents' knowledge.

All of these items require immediate action, direct contact with the school, and possibly the help of a trained professional. We'll discuss these issues next.

Hitting the Reset Button

If your child gets into serious trouble, you'll want to deal with it right away. Where the 1-to-1 program is involved, families and schools are, by definition, involved. The possible far-reaching impact of serious trouble means that the situation needs to be handled with a thoughtful and organized approach.

First, start with the right attitude:

- Before trying to address the issues, everyone needs to be thinking clearly. This requires a sense of relative calm and trust. Problems will not be resolved or even addressed if everyone is arguing.
- The goal is to make things right.
- Don't focus only on the trouble. Your child also needs you to focus on his or her feelings (anger, fear, sadness, guilt, etc.) and the feelings of others who might be involved.
- Trouble involving the 1-to-1 device requires keeping in mind the whole picture—home, school, and perhaps the wider community.

Chapter 4   Stop!   Reset If Something Goes Wrong

There is a silver lining: The trouble is out in the open, so it can now be dealt with. Here's how to hit the reset button:

Step 1—Finding Out

How did you find out that something went wrong? Did your child come to you? Did you find out from the school or another parent? Did you snoop?

If you found out from your child, it's important first to thank him or her for coming to you. This may seem strange, but it is important to establish open communication and trust. It's always worse to hear it from someone else. Regardless of where the news came from, treat this moment tactfully because you will likely need the help of the messenger, your child, to *make things right*. Remember: Honesty and open communication between parents and children are more precious than gold.

If the news comes from another source, you also have to address the deception with your child.

Step 2—The Initial Conversation with Your Child

There will be time to sort through exactly what happened. Find a way to have an initial conversation that has a large dose of empathy for your child. Is he or she scared, hurt, sad, angry, or embarrassed? When you recognize his or her feelings (without making too many judgments), it will be easier for your child to open up.

Step 3—Information Gathering

Once your child senses that you are not an adversary, you can begin a collaborative process of gathering information. In a 1-to-1 program, this means thinking about the reality of a digital culture where information moves quickly. This should be done without too much judgment. If you are looking for a motto, Google the name "Joe Friday" and go for "the facts, just the facts."

Step 4—Stopping the Trouble

What happens next depends on the nature of the trouble. If the trouble continues online, it may be necessary to take a break from specific sites or the 1-to-1 device.

If you have to take away the 1-to-1 device, it is most realistic to see it less as a punishment and more as a way to stop the trouble. You may also have to work with the school's principal or members of the technology department to let them know what happened and to figure out how your child can do schoolwork without the 1-to-1 device.

Step 5—Making Things Right

When a child gets into serious trouble, he or she has made a series of poor choices that caused harm to self, another person, or property. Once you have gathered all of the facts and related information, know the choices, and have stopped the trouble, you have everything needed to reset. Backtrack along the string of poor choices and think together as a family about what next steps would be best to give your child the experience of restoring safety, trust, and respect to all parties involved.

This should not be done in a way that shames your child (demands for public apologies can shame children to the point that they become depressed or alienated from their families or school). Some of the most effective techniques for making things right occur quietly and do not require any communication beyond the family or specific people involved.

Step 6—Return with Restrictions (Reset)

After a reasonable length of time has passed, you can slowly begin to lift restrictions on the ways that your child uses the 1-to-1 device. If you involved the school, keep the school informed about this process. Expect your child to be somewhat confused about distinguishing between social life and schoolwork on the 1-to-1 device. Invite a healthy dialogue about the gray areas of having a 1-to-1 device at home. Revise or start over with the 1-to-1 agreements in this guidebook (the forms in Appendix A, especially Forms A.2 and A.3, and their descriptions in Chapter 1).

Conclusion

After spending many hours thinking about 1-to-1 programs, I am happy to report that I continue to feel a sense of optimism about their impact on schools, kids, and families. I feel this sense of optimism for current 1-to-1 programs and for schools that will adopt these programs in the future. This guidebook is focused on the home side of school-issued laptops and tablets, and this is the area where I feel the greatest sense of optimism.

My optimism starts with the dialogue that the 1-to-1 program creates between home and school about the health and well-being of kids in the digital age. To truly address the privacy and safety concerns of new technologies, a child's whole world needs to be considered; local government officials, businesses (including websites), schools, educators, communities, and families all need to work together. Digital tools like the 1-to-1 device blur boundaries and disrupt institutions, affecting the safety and privacy of children and families. We need to address these issues on multiple levels. The link that the 1-to-1 program creates between home and school is an important step in this direction.

Educators and parents working together is a small aspect of the systemic changes needed in our educational system, but the power of this collaboration should not be underestimated. One of the biggest challenges to youth identity formation in the digital age is providing kids the perspective necessary to better see the effects of their actions in a digital world. We can only expect kids to make good decisions about their online lives when we have expanded their world view beyond their peer group and social lives. 1-to-1 schools that use the tools of the 21st century to educate their students are making an important statement about identity formation. They are saying that online identity can be multifaceted and should include academic strengths and positive interests. My hope is that parents will use this book to support their children in exploring the positive ways the 1-to-1 device can be used to build a more solid sense of self.

Conclusion

The 1-to-1 device comes home with a set of unique challenges that can actually bring families closer together when parents and children communicate honestly and thoughtfully. One of the main takeaways from this guidebook is that while the 1-to-1 program disrupts the boundary between home and school, which can cause conflicts, it can also present opportunities for families to learn the skills necessary to manage during times of disruption. This book aims to provide parents with reasonable perspectives and practical tools that can help them find greater enjoyment of life with their children during times of change. When parents and their children work out mutually beneficial agreements about use of 1-to-1 devices at home, children will learn how to take on increasingly higher levels of responsibility—for the device itself, for balancing study time with game and social time, and for the ethical choices they make.

I believe the bridge that the 1-to-1 program creates between home and school will expand our definitions of how kids are educated and the ways that they learn. I see the potential for parents to become valuable educational resources, as their knowledge and expertise can be more readily available to influence not only their own children, but also other students in the wider school community.

By changing the idea that school learning can only happen within the four walls of the school building and during school hours, we can provide kids with a far richer education. My personal hope is that these educational changes will open up greater avenues for teaching social and emotional skills at home and school.

Appendix A

Forms and Checklists

This guidebook has seven reproducible checklists and four reproducible forms designed for parent use. The checklists appear in Chapter 2. The forms appear in this appendix.

Name of Checklist	Chapter 2 Location
Parental Control, Filtering, and Monitoring Software Checklist	Checklist 1, p. 25
Downloading Media Checklist	Checklist 2, p. 31
Video Sites Checklist	Checklist 3, p. 36
Social Networks Checklist	Checklist 4, p. 42
Video Games Checklist	Checklist 5, p. 49
Chatting Checklist (Video, Voice, and Text)	Checklist 6, p. 55
Ergonomics and Sleep Checklist	Checklist 7, p. 62

Name of Form	Appendix A Location
School and Parent Guidelines and Responsibilities for the 1-to-1 Device	Form A.1, p. 89
Child Guidelines and Responsibilities Agreement for the 1-to-1 Device	Form A.2, p. 92
1-to-1 Family Agreement	Form A.3, p. 95
Record for the 1-to-1 Device	Form A.4, p. 100

Forms A.1, A.2, and A.3 are discussed in Chapter 1. Filled-out samples of Forms A.1 and A.2 appear in Chapter 1 as Figures 1.1 and 1.2. Additional cells are provided for adding further responsibilities (Form A.1) or further aggreements (Form A.2).

Appendix A Forms and Checklists

It is best to complete the checklists and review the entire guidebook before filling out the family agreement, Form A.3, with your child, together, at home. Once you, the parent(s), and your child have a clearer sense of home and school responsibilities, you can help your child understand and agree to take on these responsibilities. In families with more than one child using a 1-to-1 device, each child will need to fill in his or her own agreements (Forms A.2 and A.3) with parent(s).

A fourth form, A.4, is for recording important information about the school-issued 1-to-1 device. Form A.4 is meant to help you gather and organize important information about the device. This is information that you will want to have if something should go wrong with the 1-to-1 device or should it get lost, stolen, or broken. This form should be filled out as soon as the device comes home or shortly after it has been received. Many schools will provide the information in this form at a parent education evening. If your school does not provide an evening to review information about the 1-to-1 device, set up a time to talk to the person at school who is in charge of the 1-to-1 program. You may want to review this information with your child, but it is not necessary to fill out Forms A.1 or A.4 with your child present.

Form A.1 School and Parent Guidelines and Responsibilities for the 1-to-1 Device

School and Parent Guidelines and Responsibilities

Physical Care and Maintenance of the Equipment

School	Parent	Responsibility	Notes
		Provide an acceptable use policy (AUP) for taking care of the equipment.	
		Provide a protective case for the equipment.	
		Provide a policy for adding additional software or hardware.	
		Provide a policy on decorating the 1-to-1 device.	
		Provide a policy on charging the 1-to-1 device to ensure that it will have a full battery during the school day.	
		Provide tips to encourage students to bring a fully charged 1-to-1 device to school each day.	
		Provide information and policies about backing up student work.	

Continued

Appendix A   Forms and Checklists

Form A.1 School and Parent Guidelines and Responsibilities   *Continued*

Student and Family Social and Emotional Support

School	Parent	Responsibility	Notes
		Provide an acceptable use policy (AUP) that covers social behavior and the 1-to-1 device.	
		Provide students with opportunities to learn about Internet safety and digital citizenship.	
		Provide a parent education evening about social and emotional issues and the 1-to-1 device.	Date & Time:
		Provide ongoing opportunities for a dialogue between parents and the school to discuss the impacts of the 1-to-1 device on home life.	
		Provide a policy about other people (siblings, friends, parents) using the equipment.	
		Provide a policy about how the laptop/tablet will be used during school breaks (lunch, recess, etc.).	

Form A.1 School and Parent Guidelines and Responsibilities *Continued*

Specific Issues and Challenges			
School	Parent	Responsibility	Notes
		Provide parental control, filtering, and/or monitoring software.	
		Provide information about when the 1-to-1 device can be used (e.g., at night after bedtime, on weekends).	
		Provide information and guidelines about how much time a student should spend using the 1-to-1 device per school day and on weekends for school-related projects.	
		Provide guidelines about what types of videos, music, and text constitute explicit content (i.e., sexual, violent, profane) and rules about storing or viewing this content on the 1-to-1 device.	
		Provide guidelines about chatting (video or text) and the 1-to-1 device.	
		Provide guidelines about playing video games on the 1-to-1 device.	
		Provide guidelines about using social network sites on the 1-to-1 device.	
		Provide information about ergonomics and avoiding repetitive stress injuries.	

Form A.2 Child Guidelines and Responsibilities Agreement for the 1-to-1 Device

Child Guidelines and Responsibilities Agreement

Physical Care and Maintenance of the Equipment

Child (initials)	Agreement	Notes (details, date, parent initials)
_____	Understands and agrees to follow acceptable use policy on taking care of the equipment.	
_____	Understands and agrees to follow policy on adding additional software or hardware.	
_____	Understands and agrees to follow policy on decorating the 1-to-1 device.	
_____	Understands and agrees to follow policy on charging the 1-to-1 device to ensure that it will have a full battery during the school day.	
_____	Understands and agrees to follow policies on backing up student work.	

Form A.2 Child Guidelines and Responsibilities Agreement *Continued*

Student Social and Emotional Support		
Child (initials)	**Agreement**	**Notes (details, date, parent initials)**
_____	Understands and agrees to follow acceptable use policy that covers social behavior and the 1-to-1 device.	
_____	Understands and agrees to follow policy on other people (siblings, friends, parents) not being allowed to use the equipment.	
_____	Understands and agrees to follow policy on how the laptop/tablet will be used during school breaks (lunch, recess, etc.).	

Continued

Form A.2 Child Guidelines and Responsibilities Agreement *Continued*

Specific Issues and Challenges		
Child (initials)	**Agreement**	**Notes (details, date, parent initials)**
_____	Understands and agrees to how parental control, filtering, and/or monitoring software will be used.	
_____	Understands and agrees to times when the 1-to-1 device can be used (such as at night after bedtime, on weekends).	
_____	Understands and agrees to follow school guidelines on how much time a student should spend using the 1-to-1 device per school day and on weekends for school-related projects.	
_____	Agrees to follow school guidelines on what videos, music, and text constitute explicit content and to follow rules about storing or viewing this content on the 1-to-1 device.	
_____	Agrees to guidelines on chatting (video or text) and the 1-to-1 device.	
_____	Agrees to guidelines on playing video games on the 1-to-1 device.	
_____	Agrees to guidelines on using social network sites on the 1-to-1 device.	
_____	Understands and agrees to follow guidelines on ergonomics and avoiding repetitive stress injuries.	

Form A.3 1-to-1 Family Agreement

1-to-1 Child and Parent Agreement

This agreement is going to help our family get the most out of being a part of
_____'s [child's name] school's 1-to-1 program.

I (we), _____ [parent name(s)], understand that the laptop or tablet was issued to you, _____ [child's name], *by your school,* and much of the responsibility to use it wisely is going to be up to you.

We are, however, in this together. Having a laptop or tablet will impact our family because it comes home with you at the end of each school day, and it will play a big role in your social and school life. Also, when you are using the 1-to-1 device, you are representing not only yourself but also your school and family. If a serious situation should arise where rules are broken while you are using the laptop or tablet, your parent(s), school, and you will all be responsible for helping you to make it right.

It is less likely that things will go wrong if we are clear about what we want from each other when it comes to the 1-to-1 device.

I (we), your parent(s)

- want to see you work up to your potential in school.
- want you to have positive relationships with peers, teachers, and friends.
- want our time together as a family not to be spent arguing.
- want you to feel comfortable coming to us if you need help.

Parent Responsibilities

I (we), your parent(s), have been researching the benefits and the challenges that families face when being part of a 1-to-1 program, and I am (we are) ready to do my (our) part to make the 1-to-1 program work well for everyone in our family.

When you are at school,

- your school lets you know how to use the 1-to-1 appropriately.

Continued

Form A.3 1-to-1 Family Agreement *Continued*

When you are away from school (at home, at friends' or relatives' houses, at after-school activities, etc.),

- I (we) will clearly communicate our rules and help you to understand what you can and cannot do on the 1-to-1 device.
- I (we) will do research to make sure our rules are reasonable.
- I (we) may consult with your school about how to make the 1-to-1 program work effectively at home.
- if I (we) decide to consult with your school, I (we) will come to you first to discuss concerns with you and ask for your ideas.
- if you feel that our rules unfairly restrict your social or school life, I (we) will listen to your concerns and help find ways to provide you with what you need.

By signing this agreement, I (we), _____ [parent name(s)], will work hard to live up to my (our) responsibilities. If you feel that I am not (we are not) living up to my (our) responsibilities, we can sit down with this agreement and reevaluate it at any time.

Child's Responsibilities

It is important to me, _____ [child's name], that I use my school-issued 1-to-1 device responsibly. I am aware that the laptop or tablet is different from all other digital devices that I may own because it comes from school. It is also different because it comes home with me at the end of each school day. For these reasons, when using the 1-to-1 device, I am representing not only myself but also my school and family. I want to get the most out of having a laptop or tablet, and I see that it is important to use it with a sense of safety, trust, and respect.

The safety principles for using the 1-to-1 device are not that different from the ones in my everyday life:

- I know not to visit places online that might put me into dangerous or embarrassing situations.
- I know to avoid communicating with people who are interested in conversations that could lead to dangerous, embarrassing, or inappropriate situations.

Form A.3 1-to-1 Family Agreement *Continued*

- I know not to view material or engage with other people in ways that I am not ready to handle.
- I know that I need to take breaks from the laptop or tablet and do other activities besides being in front of a laptop or tablet screen.
- I know that the laptop or tablet travels with me from home to school and everywhere in between, but this does not mean that my behavior will be the same everywhere. I will behave in the most appropriate ways in all of these places, showing respect for my parents, my teachers, my friends and relatives, and myself.

I understand that I can demonstrate that I deserve greater trust when I use my 1-to-1 device appropriately. I recognize that with greater trust, there are fewer arguments at home. I also understand that as my parents see they can trust me, I will gain more freedom to make my own choices. Here are some ways I can gain parent trust:

- Clearly communicate how much time I need to spend on the 1-to-1 device.
- Clearly communicate how I will spend that time.
- Stick to the amount of time I said I needed or clearly communicate why I need more time.
- Stick to the way I said I would spend my time or clearly communicate why I am changing how I spend my time.

The 1-to-1 device allows me opportunities to communicate not only with my friends and school, but also with people of all ages throughout the entire world. This means that I will be making choices about how I communicate to a wide range of people while using the 1-to-1 device.

I want to communicate with respect, so

- I will be very careful not to allow images or information about myself that are embarrassing or degrading to be placed on the Internet.
- I will avoid places/situations where people are treating others in ways that could hurt feelings or reputations.
- I will not represent my school and family in ways that will bring embarrassment or hurt feelings to them or to me.

Continued

Form A.3 1-to-1 Family Agreement *Continued*

- I will treat the 1-to-1 device in ways that ensure it will not break and ensure it will always be charged and able to function properly at home and at school.

By signing this agreement, I, _____ [child's name], am committing to work hard to live up to the responsibilities that come with my 1-to-1 device. I am entitled to revisit these responsibilities at any time, and I will agree to requests by my parent(s) to sit down and reevaluate this agreement.

Family's Responsibilities

There are challenges that come with being part of a 1-to-1 program that require our family to work together. These challenges require a willingness to change some of our old patterns and commit to a fresh start when it comes to the 1-to-1 program.

Homework vs. Hanging out or Playtime:

- Our family recognizes that having the 1-to-1 device changes some of the ways that studying and homework take place.
- Our family understands that sometimes it is necessary to turn off distractions and to focus on work and on family time together (whether that is homework, chores around the house, or times we agree to spend together as a family).
- Our family also understands that the line between learning and playing is less clear with the 1-to-1 device. Thus, the same tools that are used for play (digital social networks, video games, watching videos, etc.) may also be used to do school assignments.
- Our family will work to build a sense of trust that wise decisions are being made about how schoolwork gets done.
- Our family will take time to figure out how best to make time to study and time to play/hang out.

Screen Time (the time kids are engaged with digital technologies):

- Our family is aware that having the 1-to-1 device is likely going to mean more screen time.
- Our family is also aware that it is important to focus on what is being done with screen time as well as the amount of screen time.
- Our family will take the time to discuss how screen time is being spent.

Form A.3 1-to-1 Family Agreement *Continued*

- Our family will make sure that that there are enough activities that take place away from screens.
- Our family will work together to figure out how to ensure that there is time for a full range of experiences beyond the 1-to-1 device.

Privacy:

- Our family acknowledges that everyone needs some privacy.
- Our family will work together to find an appropriate amount of privacy with regard to the 1-to-1 device.
- Our family recognizes that the 1-to-1 device from school is different from all of the other laptops, tablets, and/or computers that our family already owns and may require different privacy rules.
- Our family will find ways to demonstrate that the 1-to-1 device is being used responsibly and allow for greater freedom when responsibility is demonstrated.
- Our family will avoid snooping into each other's lives and be clear about the information that is needed to ensure that the 1-to-1 device is being used responsibly.

By signing this agreement, we, _____
[parent name(s) and child's name], will work hard to live up to our responsibilities. If anyone in our family feels that we are not living up to our responsibilities, we can sit down and reevaluate this agreement at any time.

_____
Parent signature(s)   Date

_____
Child's signature   Date

Notes: _____
_____
_____
_____

Form A.4 Record for the 1-to-1 Device

School-Issued 1-to-1 Device Record
Student name:
Parent name:
School name:
Type of device:
Operating system:
Serial #:

Person to contact for technical questions:
    Email:
    Phone:

Person to contact for behavioral questions:
    Email:
    Phone:

Cost of device:
Cost of insurance:
Cost of deductible:
Date to be handed out:
Date device comes home:
Date device is to be returned:
In the event that the device gets broken or stolen:
Notes:

Appendix B

Resources

General Background Resources

I have found a handful of sources to be particularly helpful in my work with families who are adjusting to the new digital landscape and in writing this guidebook. These are reliable places for balanced information about the impacts of new technology on the social, emotional, and cognitive development of kids and families. Also included are resources that have influenced my thinking about family communication on difficult topics. I have found these techniques particularly helpful when discussing guidelines for use of the 1-to-1 device with parents and students because they focus on finding common ground.

Technology

Each week journalist Anne Collier of NetFamilyNews.org discusses the biggest stories happening in the world of kids and technology. She provides thoughtful, insightful analysis that expands stories about kids and technology past the headlines. Collier's writing provides a balanced perspective and is clearly influenced by her own experience as a parent. If you are going to consult one place to better understand a big story about kids and technology, see www.netfamilynews.org. Her work also appears in SafeKids.com, the Internet-safety site she codirects with Larry Magid (www.connectsafely.org/safety-tips-and-advice.html).

I find Common Sense Media (www.commonsensemedia.org) to be a reliable source when it comes to reviewing the appropriateness of media for kids from early childhood through adolescence. They also do a good job with practical advice for parents and educators. If you are wondering when is the right time to introduce a new technology (such as a cell phone, a video game console, etc.) or want to get a better of sense of the pros and cons of a particular video game, movie, app, or website, Common Sense Media is very helpful.

Appendix B   Resources

Technology Research

It is easy to find research about kids and technology that makes a news story sound more sensational or hypes a new product or service. It is harder to find research that seems to capture the trends while providing an accurate picture of how kids are using new technologies. I find the Pew Internet & American Life Project (http://pewinternet.org) to be the best place to get accurate, consistent, and timely research about families, kids, and technology.

1-to-1 Information

Matt Levinson's book, *From Fear to Facebook* (ISTE, 2010), is written from the perspective of a school administrator. Levinson narrates one school's journey as it launched a 1-to-1 laptop program. The book offers thoughtful and realistic views on the challenges and benefits of integrating technology into schools. The narrative form contributes to making this book an easy read and a great source if you are curious about how starting a 1-to-1 program can affect schools, teachers, students, and parents.

Communicating with Kids and Teens

As a therapist, I am always looking for resources to help families with communication skills. I tend to like books and techniques that capture the kinds of real conflicts that I hear in my office and that provide practical tips for alternative communication strategies. It would be unfair to expect any book or technique of this kind to be perfect because our communication styles vary widely, but the following are examples of books and techniques I have found helpful.

Ross W. Greene is the author of *The Explosive Child* and *Lost at School* and the originator of the Collaborative Problem Solving (CPS) approach. His website, Lives in the Balance (www.livesinthebalance.org), contains information on his strategies for dealing with angry, defiant, and oppositional children. For more details on Greene's methods, see *The Explosive Child: A New Approach for Understanding and Parenting Easily Frustrated, Chronically Inflexible Children* (Harper, 2010) and *Lost at School: Why Our Kids with Behavioral Challenges Are Falling Through the Cracks and How We Can Help Them* (Simon & Schuster, 2009).

Marshall B. Rosenberg is the founder and director of educational services for the Center for Nonviolent Communication and author of numerous books. *Nonviolent Communication: A Language of Life* (Puddledancer, 2003) is a good introduction to the subject. Also see the Center for Nonviolent Communication's website (www.cnvc.org) for information on its training and materials.

Resources for Specific Issues

Online resources for specific issues (parental control, filtering, and monitoring software; downloading media; video sites; social networks; video games; video, voice, and text chatting; and ergonomics and sleep) are mentioned throughout Chapter 2 and are consolidated here for a ready reference.

Parental Control, Filtering, and Monitoring Software

Apple's Parental Controls
    www.apple.com/findouthow/mac/#parentalcontrols

Cable Companies' Parental Controls
    www.pointsmartclicksafe.org/parental-controls.html

Google's Family Safety Center
    www.google.com/goodtoknow/familysafety

OpenDNS's Parental Controls
    www.opendns.com/home-solutions

Parenting Online Kids
- www.netfamilynews.org/the-trust-factor-in-parenting-online-kids (part one)
- www.netfamilynews.org/parenting-or-digital-public-humiliation (part two)

Windows' Parental Controls
    http://windows.microsoft.com/en-US/windows-vista/Set-up-Parental-Controls

Appendix B Resources

Downloading Media

Apple Offers Parents an iTunes Allowance for Kids
  http://support.apple.com/kb/HT2105

Apple's Parental Controls for iTunes' Content
  http://support.apple.com/kb/ht1904

Common Sense Media Distinguishes Legal from Illegal Downloads
  www.commonsensemedia.org/advice-for-parents/illegal-downloads-when-sharing-becomes-stealing

Setting Allowance and Parental Controls for iTunes on iPhones and iPads
  www.quepublishing.com/articles/article.aspx?p=1917164

Video Sites

Apps Limit Digital Distractions to Help Users Stay on Task
  http://u.com/articles/6969/10-Online-Tools-for-Better-Attention-Focus

Vimeo's Community Guidelines
  http://vimeo.com/help/guidelines

YouTube's Community Guidelines
  www.youtube.com/t/community_guidelines

Resources: Social Networks

Common Sense Media Names Social Networking Sites for Younger Kids
  www.commonsensemedia.org/website-lists/social-networking-kids

A Facebook Guide for Parents
  www.connectsafely.org/pdfs/fbparents.pdf

Facebook's Methods for Reporting and Addressing Abuse
  www.facebook.com/help/263149623790594

Facebook's Online Safety Basics for Parents
  www.facebook.com/safety/groups/parents

Resources: Video Games

Apple's Parental Controls for Kids' Time on Computer or Apps
www.apple.com/findouthow/mac/#parentalcontrols

Common Sense Media's Advice for Parents on Educational and Entertainment Apps
www.commonsensemedia.org/advice-for-parents/
apps-101-what-know-you-download

Common Sense Media Advises Setting Screen-Time Limits
www.commonsensemedia.org/advice-for-parents/
dont-touch-dial-tips-limiting-screen-time

ESRB Video Games' Ratings
www.esrb.org/ratings

ESRB Video Games' Ratings Explained on Wikipedia
http://en.wikipedia.org/wiki/Entertainment_Software_Rating_Board

How to Make Parental Controls More Effective
http://netsecurity.about.com/od/security101/a/8-Ways-To-Kid-Proof-Your-Internet-Parental-Controls.htm

Windows' Parental Controls for Kids' Time on Computer or Apps
http://windows.microsoft.com/en-US/windows7/products/features/parental-controls

Resources: Video, Voice, and Text Chatting

Apple's Video Chat Software
www.apple.com/ios/facetime

Google's Chat Features
http://support.google.com/chat/bin/answer.py?hl=en&answer=161934

Facebook's Chat Features
www.facebook.com/help/332952696782239

Facebook's Video Calling Chat Feature
www.facebook.com/videocalling

Skype's Video Chat Features
http://about.skype.com/product.html

Resources: Ergonomics and Sleep

Apple's Ergonomics Tips
www.apple.com/about/ergonomics

Ergonomically Healthy Posture at the Computer
www.youtube.com/watch?v=TGx8yfiNvzk

Microsoft's Ergonomics Tips
www.microsoft.com/hardware/en-us/support/healthy-computing-guide

Sleep Deficits May Impair Kids' Cognitive Functioning
http://nymag.com/news/features/38951

Standing Desks
www.nytimes.com/2012/12/02/business/stand-up-desks-gaining-favor-in-the-workplace.html?_r=0

Stretching App
www.stretchclock.com/more

Teens Need More Sleep!
www.pbs.org/wgbh/pages/frontline/shows/teenbrain/from/sleep.html

Technology, Responsibility and Your Children

Technology is changing the way children engage with the world.

Educators and parents rely on ISTE's HomePage Books to provide guidance and help them teach children how to be responsible digital citizens.

Find the latest ed tech books focused on the topics that matter most to educators and parents at iste.org/store.

iste.org/store